THE LETTERS OF ADAM OF PERSEIGNE

CISTERCIAN STUDIES SERIES: NUMBER NUMBER TWENTY-ONE

THE LETTERS OF
Adam of Perseigne

VOLUME I

Translated by
Grace Perigo

Introduction by
Thomas Merton

α

Cistercian Publications
www.cistercianpublications.org

LITURGICAL PRESS
Collegeville, Minnesota
www.litpress.org

A Cistercian Publications title published by Liturgical Press

Cistercian Publications
Editorial Offices
161 Grosvenor Street
Athens, Ohio 45701
www.cistercianpublications.org

This translation is based on the edition prepared by Jean Bouvet and published in the series Sources chrétiennes: Textes monastiques d'occident, IV (Paris: Cerf, 1960).

Ecclesiastical permission to publish this volume was given by Bernard Flanagan, Bishop of Worcester, 1 December 1975.

© Cistercian Publications, Inc., 1976. © 2008 by Order of Saint Benedict, Collegeville, Minnesota. All rights reserved. © "A Feast of Freedom" by Merton Legacy Trust. No part of this book may be used or reproduced in any manner whatsoever, except brief quotations in reviews, without written permission of Liturgical Press, Saint John's Abbey, PO Box 7500, Collegeville, MN 56321-7500. Printed in the United States of America.

Library of Congress Catalog Card Number: 76-15486

ISBN 978-0-87907-196-7 (paperback)

TABLE OF CONTENTS

Abbreviations vii

The Feast of Freedom
   by Thomas Merton 3

Letter I 49
Letter II 57
Letter III 65
Letter IV 91
Letter V 97
Letter VI 111
Letter VII 122
Letter VIII 129
Letter IX 133
Letter X 139
Letter XI 151
Letter XII 161
Letter XIII 165
Letter XIV 174
Letter XV 194

ABBREVIATIONS

Scriptural references and abbreviations are taken from The Jerusalem Bible

Ac	Acts	Ml	Malachi
Co	Corinthians	Mk	Mark
Col	Colossians	Mt	Matthew
Dt	Deuteronomy	P	Peter
Eph	Ephesians	Ph	Phillipians
Est	Esther	Pr	Proverbs
Ex	Exodus	Ps	Psalms
Ga	Galatians	Qo	Ecclesiastes
Gn	Genesis	Rm	Romans
Heb	Hebrews	Rv	Revelation
Is	Isaiah	Si	Ecclesiasticus
Jb	Job	Sg	Song of Songs
Jl	Joel	Tt	Titus
Jm	James	Ws	Wisdom
Jn	John		
K	Kings	LXX	Septuagint
Lk	Luke	Vulg.	Vulgate
Lv	Leviticus		

GENERAL ABBREVIATIONS

CF	Cistercian Fathers series. Spencer; Washington; Kalamazoo, 1969–
CSEL	Corpus Scriptorum Ecclesiasticorum Latinorum. Vienna, 1866–
OB	*Sancti Bernardi Opera*, edd. J. Leclercq and H.M. Rochais. Rome, 1957–
PL	Patrologiae cursus completus, series latina, ed. J.-P. Migne. Paris, 1844–64.
RB	Saint Benedict's Rule for Monasteries
SC	Sources chrétiennes series. Paris, 1941–

CISTERCIAN WORKS CITED

Aelred of Rievaulx

Iesu	*De Iesu puero duodenni* (On Jesus at the Age of Twelve)
Spec car	*Speculum caritatis* (The Mirror of Charity)

Bernard of Clairvaux

Gra	*De gratia et libero arbitrio* (On Grace and Free Choice)
Miss	*Homilia super missus est in laudibus virginis matris*
V Nat	*Sermones in vigilia nativitatis domini*

William of St Thierry

Contemp	*De contemplando deo* (On contemplating God)
Med	*Meditativae orationes* (Meditations)
Nat am	*De natura et dignitate amoris* (The Nature and Dignity of Love)
Phys corp	*Physica humani corporis (De natura corporis et animae)*

THE FEAST OF FREEDOM

by THOMAS MERTON

MONASTIC FORMATION ACCORDING TO
ADAM OF PERSEIGNE

THE FEAST OF FREEDOM

MONASTIC FORMATION ACCORDING TO ADAM OF PERSEIGNE

AT THE END OF THE TWELFTH CENTURY and the beginning of the thirteenth the Cistercian Abbey of Perseigne in Normandy had for its abbot a man of learning and sanctity who, like so many other Cistercians of his day, played an important part in the religious life of the age. His reputation for learning and holiness gradually won him an ever-increasing influence first in other monasteries of the Order, then in abbeys of the Benedictines and in various Charterhouses. At the same time his advice in spiritual matters was sought on every side, and he became what we might call today the 'spiritual director' of many great secular and ecclesiastical personages, the most famous of whom was Richard Coeur de Lion.

This future director of kings was himself a man of very humble social origins. The son of a serf of the Count of Champagne, he had been born somewhere around the time when the monastery of Perseigne was founded (1145). We do not know where he acquired his considerable store of education

—probably in one of the cathedral cities of Champagne: Troyes, Rheims or Sens. He was ordained to the secular clergy and found himself early in favor in the court of Champagne where he shone, among other things, as a poet writing in the vernacular. He was the chaplain of the Countess of Champagne.

Although the details of Adam's life are very uncertain, we know from his own avowal that he had passed from the secular clergy to a monastery of Canons Regular, thence to the Black Monks (or Benedictines) and finally to the Order of Cîteaux. We do not know the reason for these wanderings, except that he was looking for a life of complete renunciation and prayer, and that he finally chose the Cistercians because of their special devotion to the Blessed Virgin Mary. It is thought that he entered the Order at Pontigny.

By 1188, or perhaps even 1183, Adam had become abbot of Perseigne, in Normandy, the monastery where the famous Abbé de Rancé was to make his novitiate, in the seventeenth century, before assuming his office as regular abbot of La Grande Trappe.

Although Adam of Perseigne was not another Bernard of Clairvaux either in his contemplation or in his activity, he was nevertheless destined to live a life reminiscent of the great saint who dominated the twelfth century. The needs of the Church called him frequently forth from the silence of the cloister. Perseigne, being in

Normandy, was under the protection of the Plantagenets, the reigning house of England. Several charters remain to bear witness to the friendship of Henry II and Richard I (Coeur de Lion) for the monastery, and it was in this way that Adam became a trusted advisor to the second of these kings.

One of the most important missions with which Adam of Perseigne was entrusted by the Church was that of handling the 'difficult case' of Joachim of Fiora. Joachim, a Cistercian abbot in Italy whose doctrines came under censure after his death, was a powerful and doubtless disturbing influence in the Church at the end of the Middle Ages. His doctrine of the coming of a New Age, the 'Age of the Holy Ghost' started one of those 'prophetic' movements characteristic of the time. We do not know precisely what Adam was supposed to do with Joachim, or to what extent he succeeded. He was in Italy in 1195, and was back again in France the following year.

In the hard years of famine that closed the twelfth century, Adam of Perseigne joined the great crusade of charity led by Foulques de Neuilly to feed the poor and to convert souls. In 1200, his name is among those designated to help preach a less metaphorical Crusade. Like St Bernard, Adam sent men off to fight the Holy War for Jerusalem. It is doubtful whether he embarked with the Crusaders, and he is not mentioned in Villehardouin's *Chronicle*,

The Feast of Freedom

though other Cistercian abbots went with the expedition. In 1208, Adam was charged by the Holy See to negotiate peace between Philippe Auguste and John Lackland. During the last years of his life, at his own request, he was spared such missions as these and was permitted to remain more often and for longer periods in the peace of the cloister. One of the few events of his declining years was the foundation of a convent of Cistercian nuns under his tutelage. The abbess was a nun who had been for a long time under his direction and who had received many letters from his hand. One of the last recorded events in his history was that he was penanced by the General Chapter of 1218 for allowing laypersons to be buried in the church of Perseigne. He had also been penanced once before for an 'excessive' spirit of hospitality—when he had allowed cheese and eggs to be served to his guests on a Friday! He died about 1221.

Not all Adam's writings have yet been published. There can be found in Migne's Patrology* a representative selection of letters and his *Mariale,* a collection of homilies on the Blessed Virgin which rates a high place in the Cistercian literature of the Middle Ages. A volume of his letters has appeared in the French series, *Sources Chretiennes.** Adam's doctrine is typical of school of St Bernard, but is not without a character and vitality of its own. The pages that follow, without pretending to be an exhaustive study of the theme of monastic

*PL 211

*SC 66. [on which this translation is based—ed.]

formation as it was developed by him, will nevertheless provide an introduction to his thought and to his 'spirituality'.

Like so many of the Cistercian Fathers, Adam was a penetrating observer of life and possessed a profound intuitive knowledge of the human soul. But he was also and above all a theologian who knew God in his revealed word. His knowledge of the Scriptures, far from being mere piety or dry pedantry, entered deeply into the very substance of his every day life so that, like St Bernard, Adam viewed and experienced everything in a scriptural atmosphere. He heard God's word in everything that happened. He was one who saw all things, and particularly the monastic life itself, centered in the mystery of Christ. Because of this unity of outlook, Adam's theology of the spiritual life is not merely a collection of devout abstractions or a synthesis of ideas: it is a *sapientia,* a wisdom which is rooted in life. His theology is centered in the knowledge of Christ living in the Church and exercising his divine action upon souls through the Holy Spirit. Hence when Adam speaks of the formation of Cistercian novices he does not merely talk about the acquisition of virtues or exterior discipline (although these also find their place in his theology), he speaks of life in Christ, life in the Spirit, Christ living in us. He speaks of 'the new man who is created according to God in justice and the sanctity of truth.'

True, light, holiness, grace—all these are manifestations of Christ living in our souls.

To form a Cistercian novice is then to draw out the inner spiritual form implanted in his soul by grace: to educate—that is to say, to 'bring out'—Christ in him. It is not a matter of imposing on the novice a rigid and artificial form from without, but to encourage the growth of life and the radiation of light within his soul, until this life and light gain possession of his whole being, inform all his actions with grace and liberty, and bear witness to Christ living in him.

Adam's view of the Cistercian life is, then, characterized by its sanity, its breadth of view, its depth, its organic wholeness. It ignores and rejects nothing that is good. It takes account of the whole man, called to find his place in the whole Christ. It is realistic, simple, supremely spiritual, that is to say, attuned to the inspirations of the Holy Spirit. It is based on the great and fundamental truths of the Christian life—our union with Christ in his mysteries, through the mediation of Our Lady. The asceticism of Adam of Perseigne is based, like that of St Benedict, on silence, humility, obedience, and love. It is an asceticism in which the virtues are not just virtues but are, precisely, the virtues of Christ in us. We acquire them not by seeking virtue so much as by seeking him.

THE NEW LIFE

The most characteristic of the monastic vows is the vow of conversion of manners (*conversio morum*, or *conversatio morum*). This vow, which contains implicitly the obligations of poverty and chastity, is something more than a promise to tend to perfection. It is at once more concrete and more all embracing. It is an irrevocable consecration to a *new life* in Christ, by which one leaves behind the 'old man' by responding as far as he is able, within his own limitations, to the action of the Holy Spirit in his life.

The 'monastic formation' is then not simply the superimposition of a few religious routines upon a subject who remains unchanged: it means the transformation of the monk himself—his transformation in Christ. And this is a matter of 'life'—that is to say of an immanent spiritual principle. To give oneself over to this new life is to 'do penance' in the full sense of the word, that is to say, to 'change' (*metanoiein*) completely from within. Such is the traditional concept of the monastic vocation, and it is on this concept that Adam's teaching is based.

The postulant who knocks at the monastery gate comes from the world deformed. He is spiritually 'sick' and needs to be 'healed' by grace. This deformity of the old man must give way to the 'splendor' of the new man, a new form, the likeness of Christ. A novice is truly what his name implies only if he labors to 'take off the old man' and to be 'formed with the splendors of the new life'—*novae vitae splendoribus informentur.**

*PL 211:581

The *splendor novitatis* is symbolized by the white habit of Cîteaux. Adam's vivid expression contains all the optimism of the Cistercian spirit—a spirit related to the 'mysticism of light' of the Greek Fathers and influenced by St John's 'Gospel of Light'. The white monk is clad in a wedding garment. His cowl is a *vestis nuptialis*, a sign that he is invited and admitted to the wedding feast of the Lamb.

The true novice is one who is filled with the *sanctae splendor novitatis*—the 'splendor of holy newness'. The splendor of the new life consists especially in three things: chastity, love, and discipline. The function of discipline is to give to our lives an exterior splendor and elegance which manifest the interior love and purity of our hearts. ". . . the splendor and elegance of discipline; which, being blamelessly observed outwardly, is seen to be a sign of the interior condition of purity and love'.* *587
Hence we see how Adam relates exterior and interior perfection. In exterior perfection alone there is no splendor, no beauty. It is dead. It is a body without a soul. It can only be brought to life by the splendor of Christ. Love of the risen Christ and virginity are the two sources of contact with 'the Life which is the light of men.'

The novice is reformed 'unto the beauty of the new man' by the 'study of a stricter life'—*studium correctioris vitae*. The idea contained in *correctior* is not only 'stricter' but 'truer'—more according to the mind of Christ. The *splendor novitatis* in our 'new life' gives glory to the Lamb—the new life is a radiance that proclaims his sanctity and his love for us—*splendor est et gloria novitatis.**

Ibid.

What is the deformity of the old man that has to be put away? It is a kind of madness—the *insania vanissimae vetustatis**—irrationality, vanity, deformity of the soul, the madness of an insane love—*amentia insani amoris.* As St Paul says, it is the condition of a soul 'corrupted by the desire of error'.* To become a novice is therefore to seek 'therapy' for this *amentia*—this condition of soul which makes us love what is unreal.

*615

*Eph 4:22

> Let him who desires to become a novice turn his heart away from the great vanity of the old man; unless, the madness of this insane love having first been removed, he shall have become sound of mind, he will not otherwise be able to engage in the new study of wisdom.*

*PL 211:615

Like St Bernard, Adam wishes first of all to restore to man the natural purity and balance of his soul before elevating him to union with God. This restoration is of course the work of grace. It makes us able to enter the *schola Christi*—the school of Divine Wisdom.

The first thing the Cistercian life must do to us is to bring us to our senses. If it does not do this, then all our apparent progress in asceticism and prayer will be deformed by the *amentia* of the old man, and the 'insanity' of his love for what is vain and unreal.

This restoration of our 'senses' is brought about by *faith, love* and *obedience*. According to Adam these are not possible unless we first resolve to forget the world we have left behind.* Contempt of the world is the beginning of our return to ourselves and to God; it precedes the second step which is entrance into the monastery and contempt of the flesh. Then comes the third step— *timor Dei*. The fourth is *confessio*—the complete acknowledgement of the truth and the final giving up of all defence of falsity in ourselves.* **Ibid.*

*Cf. 621

The 'new man' is 'created according to God in justice and the holiness of truth'.* The Holy Spirit is himself the Spirit of Truth. The Cistercian life is a life based on that interior freedom which the truth alone can give us: 'The truth shall make you free'.* Original sin, on the other hand, was the work of the 'father of lies'. It is pride, which is based on a lie by which, in one act, man becomes untrue to himself by becoming untrue to his God. This pride remains with us, and St Bernard has in many places studied its subtle work: but in all its various ways of leading us away from God, pride is always a lie. It always brings us to the feet of a false god, which is our own inordinate self-love. We cannot return to God, we cannot become new men, except in so far as we renounce this lie in ourselves. But to give up the falsity that is in us we must see that it is false. No man will cling to something that he

*Eph 4:24

*Jn 8:32

manifestly believes to be unreal. No one will defend the evil that is in himself unless for some reason he views it as a good. We have to see that what our pride believes to be good is, in fact, a very great evil. And this is very difficult. Hence the constant need to be honest with ourselves, and to grapple with the 'spirit of fiction' that is in our very blood itself, always ready to deceive us in the disguise of an angel of light.

Adam is, like so many other monks of his time, a very acute psychologist and we are often astonished by the 'modern' ring of many of his statements. True, he does not explicitly set out to explore man's unconscious mind. But he certainly recognizes that there is a deep vein of unconscious falsity in us which must become conscious, must be seen for what it is, before we can get free of its all-pervading influence in our lives. We not only have falsity within us, but we instinctively prefer it—we defend it against grace. One of the chief characteristics of the old man is his 'hypocrisy' or duplicity, the 'spirit of fiction' which prevents the light of truth, the splendor of the new life, from shining through in our souls.

It is of the greatest importance to get rid of the *spiritus fictionis,* otherwise one will be a monk in appearance only. The *spiritus fictionis* destroys the whole value of our conversion and entrance into the monastery. Some monks, says Adam, are holy only in their exterior acts. In their interior they still follow the spirit of the world—a spirit of ambition, revenge, self-complacency, love of comfort, of praise, of possessions. They are content to change the outward appearances and remain centered on themselves within.

> Having the reputation of being alive, they are dead within, for while they appear outwardly to be poor and modest, interiorly they aspire to the glory of transitory praise or to the degrees of various dignities.* *PL 211:618

The evil spirit, cast out by contempt of the world and monastic conversion, returns to find his house swept and garnished and enters in with seven worse than himself.* *Ibid.
This is what grieves the Holy Spirit*, that while pretending to be guided by him, we allow ourselves in reality to be moved by his enemy, established secretly within our souls. *Ibid.

> O supreme unhappiness, under the form of the new man to conform oneself totally to the old.... * *619

We must not imagine that it is easy altogether to avoid something of the 'spirit of fiction'. The very structure of the religious life, with its innumerable external ceremonies, and observances—with the temptation to please brethren and superiors by 'conforming'—can bring falsity and insincerity into our lives without our realizing it. To guard against this, we must not be content with our renunciation of the world by our vows, but in the fear of God we must guard the door of our hearts against the entrance of the spirit of fiction.*

Self-custody is, then, a 'most vigilant doorkeeper' who humbly and faithfully ministers to love. In Adam's own words, this intuitive, sincere awareness of our real motives acts as a guard 'who keeps out of our soul all things which might disturb the banquet of love'—*ut nihil omnino quo amoris festivitas perturbetur, admittat.** Self-knowledge is necessary to see through fiction. But it is a grace, a special gift. It cannot be merited *de condigno* by any act of ours. We must desire it and pray for it. We must try to deserve it at least by accepting the evidence of truth when it flashes upon us, not resisting and evading the accusation that we fear to face.

Falsity begins with an inordinate care of the body—seeking more than is necessary to keep us living reasonably. The traditional ascetic norms of the monastic Fathers, the *discretio patrum**, teach us that we must not deny the body what it needs, and not pamper it beyond its needs. Extreme asceticism is just as dangerous as softness and self-indulgence.

If discretion is ignored, falsity entrenches itself in the soul by the habit of sin— *usus peccandi.** This in turn gradually blinds the conscience and perverts one's whole sense of values until evil takes on the appearance of good. Thus falsity takes complete possession of the soul which defends its own sins—*defensio peccati*. Hence the special importance of self-restraint, humility, self-knowledge, and obedience, in order to defend the soul against the spirit of illusion.

But above all, the monk who has entered the monastery to seek the truth in Christ must truly and irrevocably renounce all affection for 'the world' which is the realm of falsity and illusion, under the sovereignty of the Prince of Liars. Unless a man has really given up 'the world' in its bad sense, he cannot gain that capacity for spiritual enlightenment and love which are necessary for the purification of his heart. Desire of worldly things and desire of the things of God are absolutely incompatible and they cannot reign together in one heart. One or the other must go.* Hence the necessity for an honest and uncompromising asceticism, above all for that chastity which renders the heart sensitive to spiritual love and capable of tasting the joys of contemplation.

*648

> All impurity must be cast out from our heart in order that it may be able to taste the sweetness and only joy of oneness. Let the truth of chastity (*veritas castitatis*) cast out the desires of the flesh; let the concupiscence of the eyes be kept far away by the seriousness of discipline and by the desire of inner purity. Let love of poverty and contempt of honor destroy the pride of life.*

*646

We shall see later the part played by Mary and Jesus in this work, but it is necessary at this point to observe that all this purification is not achieved by mere will-power and human effort. It is a work of divine grace, accomplished through God's love. All takes place under the eyes of God and the Blessed Virgin Mary and with her guidance.

To acquire the *mira novitas* of the new life is to share in the divine infancy of Jesus, and that means to have Mary for a mother. To avoid the 'spirit of fiction' and all the other pitfalls of life, we must dwell entirely in the love of Our Lady and receive from her the light of the new life which is the splendor of truth. She is all pure. There is in her no stain of falsity or evil. What comes to us through her love is therefore pure. It purifies our souls while forming them in the Christ-life.

Adam puts all this in a graphic and concrete form. As Jesus, the infant, had to be nourished by Mary's milk, so we who are infants in the spiritual life must also be nourished by it, and it is for this that we hunger.*

*636

What does he mean? The 'milk' with which Our Lady nourishes our lives is actual grace: light to distinguish good from evil, strength to do God's will. These we receive through her. In the order of grace we are as dependent on Mary as an infant is dependent on his natural mother. If this is true of all Christians, it is particularly true of the monk.

Adam's teaching is characteristically Cistercian in its concreteness and its positive emphasis on the happiness of our life in Christ.

> O happy newness, O new festivity which is celebrated not at the banquet table of this world but in the heaven of the pure soul.* *619

The life of the soul that has renounced all is a joyous banquet of Wisdom in which the mercy and love of God keep holiday. Here we may draw a comparison from St John of the Cross, *Living Flame*, Stanza i. (He is speaking of transforming union, but *mutatis mutandis,* and with due proportion, the same is true of lower degrees of the spiritual life.)

> When this soul is so near to God that it is transformed in the flame of Love wherein the Father and the Son and the Holy Spirit commune with it, how is it a thing incredible that it should be said to enjoy a foretaste of eternal life . . . . The delight caused in the soul by the flaming of the Holy Spirit is so sublime that it teaches the soul what is the savor of eternal life . . . . The effect of this flame is to make the soul live spiritually in God and experience the life of God, even as David says: My heart and my flesh have rejoiced in the living God . . . .
>
> Inasmuch as this is a flame of divine life it wounds the soul with the tenderness of the life of God . . . . The office of love is to wound that it may enkindle and

cause delight, so it is ever sending forth its arrow wounds like most tender sparks of delicate love, joyfully and happily exercising the arts and wiles of love....

These wounds, which are the playing of God, are the sparks of these tender touches of flame which proceed from the fire of love.

This feast of the Holy Spirit takes place in the substance of the soul where neither the devil nor the world nor sense can enter....

The more interior it is, the more abundantly and frequently and widely does God communicate Himself.... *

*Living Flame i, ed. A.A. Peers 3:120-22.

Adam does not stress the passivity of the soul, he is not speaking of purely mystical experiences. He does not speak of the feast being merely in the substance of the soul. He is not speaking only of contemplation, but also of virtuous action. But the virtuous life, the interior life, is for Adam a 'feast' of God in the depths of the soul, in which the soul is called to rejoice with God in a banquet of light and grace and peace far from the cares and deceptions of the world.

To be a monk, then, is to embrace a life in which all is designed to make us enter into this joyful and secret festivity with God who has loved us and united us to himself in Christ.

The splendor of wisdom are those virtues of the soul through which the feasts of love are continually celebrated in the secret recesses of the pure heart . . . to feasts of this kind are invited the novices, whose interior celebration is so much the more joyful, the more carefully holy fear guards the entrance to their hearts.*

*PL 211:619

The monastic ideal is therefore one of interior purity and solitude and silence in which we celebrate our new life in the Spirit and praise our heavenly Father for the mystery of our redemption in Christ.

The most important elements in this 'newness of life', he says, summarizing his thesis in Letter One, are: faith, by which we are rescued from the shadows of ignorance and incorporated in Christ; holy fear, which helps us do penance and protects our soul against the incursions of the *spiritus fictionis*; and love of wisdom, which draws us on to enter deeper into the secret life of joy with Christ.

The novice does not enter into the banquet of the interior life merely by his own good will and initiative. He needs someone to guide him in the ways of virtue and of grace. He is placed under the care of a 'Spiritual Father' whom he must obey in a spirit of faith, seeing in him the representative of God.

The Father Master must take care to prove the spirit of the novice, to see if he is really zealous for the Work of God, for obedience and humiliations, as St Benedict requires. But the Master does not expect to find these qualities already formed in the novices. It is up to him to encourage their development. He must inspire fervor in divine praise (the *Opus dei* or choral office of the monk)—especially attention to what is sung. He must make sure that the novice does not become a monk who honors God with his lips alone. With his love for truth, Adam holds this in abomination; it is hypocrisy to say what one does not mean.

The Master of Novices must teach love of obedience and humiliations. Concerning the latter Adam says:

> He who loves his brethren out of humility, is not much concerned when reproaches are heaped upon him; but rather crucifying himself with Christ, rejoices to unite himself with the ignominy of his Cross.*

*586

The spirit of prayer, the love of obedience and true humility are what St Benedict demands above all of the novice. They are the surest indication that he has come to the monastery to seek God, and not just escape from the responsibilities and difficulties of life in the world. The novice who is obedient proves that he wants to give up his own will and do the will of God. The novice who is humble gives evidence that he is not deceiving himself in trying to seek his own glory by self-exaltation in the spiritual life.

A most important element in the formation of the novice is the spiritual direction, given in an atmosphere of friendliness and love, by the Father Master: 'Friendly and frequent conversation concerning spiritual

things or the regular observances.'* Adam *Ibid.
keeps repeating the world 'friendly'—*amica*.
The direction session is a friendly conversation, marked by a 'praiseworthy familiarity'. The aim of this friendliness and sympathy is to guard the novice against discouragement and *acedia*.† The atmosphere of direction must then be one of unaffected simplicity and spontaneity, completely informal and even somewhat merry.

What is talked about in direction? The mysteries of Scripture; examples of virtue in the lives of the saints; the reward promised us in heaven, how this reward is to be gained by good works; the pains of hell and the vices which lead there; but above all, the trials and hardships of the monastic life—the *dura et aspera* (hard and painful things)*. In this matter Adam makes it *RB 58:8 clear that the Master must warn and admonish the novice concerning the *dura et aspera*. But he must avoid inflicting harsh trials and punishments on him. Adam does not recommend arbitrary and fictitious humiliations. It is the Master's duty: 'not indeed to *inflict* but to preach the *dura et aspera* through which one goes to God.'* What the Father Master should do *Ibid. is to show, demonstrate to the novice, from the Scriptures and from living examples, how it is necessary to pass through trial,

---

†*Acedia*. This complex ascetic term is not sufficiently well translated if we call it only 'spiritual sloth'. It is a kind of enervation and depression that comes when one 'goes stale' in the ascetic life, and all spiritual things tend to become repugnant and hateful. Cf. Cassian, *Institute* X.

suffering, and hardship in order to get to heaven, and how our love of Christ demands we renounce ourselves completely and abandon ourselves entirely to the way of obedience and self-denial. Real progress in the way of sanctity depends on a right understanding and a true practice of self-renunciation, in a renunciation which does not destroy our will or our nature but liberates them and consecrates them entirely to God that we may serve him fruitfully and with joy.

Finally, and this is most important, inseparable from the teaching of the *dura et aspera* is the teaching that CHRIST IS THE WAY. In other words, the negative content of this ascetic teaching is merged with the positive content which is more important: Jesus himself is with us, leads us, helps us, and sustains us in the difficulties of life. To seek them is to seek him. In finding the Cross, the love of him, we find Christ himself.

If we find Christ in our difficulties, we find joy, liberty, consolation. Hence it is that the only true hardship, the only suffering that is without fruit and which is to be avoided, is the suffering of those who travel the way of self-seeking and self-satisfaction, and who are always frustrated, never at peace, because they are not united with Christ. Those who find him are liberated from frustration and sterility. They become fruitful and are able to develop freely. Hence they are happy. In these few points Adam has outlined for us a whole directory of the Cistercian life.

CHRIST IS THE WAY

The only way to bear trials and sufferings is to find Jesus in them. What does this mean?

1. By his love, by the action of his Spirit, Jesus enters into our hearts in the midst of our trials and takes away the love of worldly things, delivers us from self-love which is the obstacle to our progress and the real source of our suffering.

Hence his action liberates, heals, and alleviates. It brings joy and strength. The inner strength which comes from Christ is something we could never attain without him. It is therefore his, it comes to us as a gift from him. Yet also it is ours, for he has given it to us, it operates in us, it is ours to use and to enjoy.

2. Jesus also and above all produces in us his own dispositions and his own love, so that doing all and suffering all as he himself does, we shall experience his victory and share his love of his Father.

Adam here remarks that the Spirit of Christ produces in us the 'three liberties' of which St Bernard speaks in the *De gratia et libero arbitrio:* freedom from sin, from necessity, from misery (Adam gives them in that order.)*   *587

3. The action of Christ produces in our souls a true love of heavenly things. This

love unites us to Christ as our Head. 'Christ is our Head. The "sense" that is in this Head is the love of heavenly things.' *Caput nostrum Christus est. Cujus capitis sensus est amor coelestium . . . .* *

*Ep 16; PL 211: 640

4. Letter 18 to the monks of Perseigne is a treatise on this action of Christ in our souls. In it, Christ appears above all as the *magister humilitatis,* the Master of Humility, not only by his teaching and example in the Gospels but by the interior action of his grace.

Christ is the fountain of living waters— the inexhaustible source of grace and wisdom.

But these waters flow only into the valley of humility. It is therefore only by humility that we learn his wisdom and acquire his virtues and fruitfulness. Humility is indeed the close friend of wisdom and of all the virtues. All our virtues must be learned from Christ. But if we do not have humility, we cannot learn any of them.

> How intimately related to heavenly Wisdom is humility, how productive of virtue, how rich in merits, how able to grasp heavenly secrets . . . .

Because humility is a channel always wide open for these living waters, it purifies the soul from every stain. It nourishes us and gives us strength for the ascetic life. It disposes our hearts for contemplation.

> Happy therefore is humility which merits to bathe in these waters lest any stain of defilement appear

or remain in it. It merits renewed strength so that in every struggle it remains steadfast.... * *644

Hence we must learn humility from Jesus:
Learn, O children, to be humble, and learn from him who is the effective teacher of this discipline, Christ.* *645

We learn to be humble from him who is humble, by imitating him, and the result is that we find peace for our hearts.

The art therefore which the Christian must learn .... the art indeed which makes the disciple of Christ is called meek humility and humble meekness.* *Ibid.

Humility, being the companion of wisdom, is also the guardian of discretion and of all the other virtues. Without humility we cannot avoid making all kinds of errors of judgment. But when we are humble (that is, when we distrust our own wisdom) our judgment is sustained and directed by the truth of Christ.

Humility is all the more secure in proportion as it is more secret—*tanto securius quanto secretius cordis disponit officia.* Not seeking to be seen and praised by men, it judges all things secretly and interiorly by the light of God's truth.* *Ep 11; PL 211: 619

The less one thinks of oneself, so much the more abundantly do graces overflow.* *Ibid.

Charming and gracious humility builds their dwellings in the soul for each and every virtue, arranges the duties of each, and nothing is done either in the bodily senses or in the affections of the soul which is not subjected to the control of this god-fearing humility.*

*620

Like St Benedict, Adam considers humility not so much in its narrow meaning as in the broad sense of a climate in which all the monastic virtues flourish, a climate of complete and trusting dependence on the grace of God.

Humility, then, guarantees right intention. It governs the passions, leading them into right channels; anger is converted into zeal for God, concupiscence is transformed into charity. Passion is sublimated and transfigured in the crucible of selflessness, over the fires of humility. Humility leads to peace, and it is the only way to contemplation. If the monk lacks humility, he can know by this sign that he is without Christ. No matter how great may be his zeal, his energy, his apparent generosity, all is empty and sterile without humility.

In a word, to summarize the Cistercian life of virtue in Christ, it can all be contained in the word *humility* as it is understood by the Benedictine tradition. Humility in this sense is something much greater than mere modesty and self-depreciation. It is a permanent disposition to live in complete submission to the deepest spiritual realities and to renounce one's own judgment at all times in order to follow the will of God. This is what it means to be taught by Christ in the Cistercian 'School of Humility'.

But the School of Christ is especially and before all else the School of the Infant Christ. In the 'emptying' of the Word in the Incarnation Adam contemplates the humility of God.

> In the meanwhile let all our philosophy be concerned with the infancy of the Incarnate Word, and the love of God toward us which this study shows us to some degree, let us strive faithfully and as far as we are able to reciprocate.*   **Ep 16:636*

Life in the cloister is a spiritual participation in the mystery of the divine infancy. The swaddling bands with which he is bound are the monastic rules:—*Fascia qua stringitur in cunabulis, sanctae est religionis districto, cujus institutione religamur in claustris.** As we meditate on the   **635* way in which he humbled himself for us we are filled with desire to be humble for love of him. As we come to understand with what great love he gave himself to be the nourishment and the life of our souls, we begin to see something of the unfathomable mystery of God's love for us. We are filled with fear, piety, strength, and all the other gifts of the Holy Spirit by the contemplation of Christ poor and helpless in the manger at Bethlehem.*   **635*

The totality of his gift of himself to us in the cradle gives us a deeper understanding of the totality of his sacrifice for us on the Cross, and inspires our hearts to give

> themselves completely to him in return:
> The entire deity poured itself out into man, all his soul it gave over to obedience. Its whole body it committed to death, even to the death of the cross, thus has the Almighty completely loved us, and it is not enough if we give back in return all that we are, all the little that we are.*

*636

The *Magister Christus,* who teaches us in his school of charity, desires by his teaching to lead us to that height of perfection which is the wisdom of the Cross, in the wisdom that consists in giving ourselves totally and completely for love of him.

The fruit of this wisdom is a union of hearts with the Incarnate Word. Here we see that Adam prepared the way for devotion to the Sacred Heart, a devotion which is deeply rooted in the Cistercian mysticism of the twelfth and thirteenth centuries. Adam teaches us that in emptying himself, in his incarnation, the Word Incarnate, coming forth from the heart of the Father, opened to us his heart in order to give us his humility, in order to show that he came to dwell in our own hearts, and therefore in order to win our hearts for himself.

> He opened his heart to us, when he emptied himself, in order to teach us by the example of his humility. He sought our heart for himself, when he showed himself to be the One who loves and dwells

in our hearts.* *Ep 18:646

A few lines later, he shows how this indwelling of Christ in our own hearts is what gives meaning to our whole spiritual life and especially to our asceticism:

> If therefore you are men of heart (*viri cordati*), if you desire to feel within you Jesus who dwells in hearts, you must guard your hearts with all care.* *Ibid.*

A *vir cordatus* is a man who has a heart, who has a strong heart—courageous and tender because it is humble. The monk, then, is *cordatus* not only because he has a man's heart, but because in his heart also beats the heart of Christ.

The presence of Christ in our hearts is kept alive by the memory of his sacred passion, and this constant thought of Jesus crucified, is intimately connected with the practice of *custodia cordis*. The light of humility and holy fear plays ever in the recesses of our soul, lighting up our actions to compare them with the sufferings and the love of Jesus. Thus we continually strive to make our lives conform to the model of his love, and in so doing we find happiness, we discover the 'freedom of devotion' with which we are always able to partake in that interior festivity, where we celebrate our union with God in the splendors of his wisdom.

> O happy soul, for whom fear has barred the paths of vice, so that with free devotion it may keep festival in these splendors of wisdom.* *Ep 11:623

This fear has nothing to do with servile anxiety. It is a form of love which makes our conscience delicate and tender. It is a purely filial fear—the dread of being separated, even for a moment, from Christ crucified dwelling in our hearts.

THE BLESSED VIRGIN AND THE CISTERCIAN LIFE

At the end of Letter 11, after speaking about the constant memory of Jesus on the Cross, Adam turns to Our Lady. He recognizes that it may prove to be too difficult for us to fix our gaze at all times on the Cross, and follow Christ Crucified without respite. In order to make this possible, he would have us look rather at Mary, who will be the source of our strength.

> If the resolve to follow this path which we have undertaken should seem difficult, let us fly to the aid of Our Virgin .... *

*623

Our union with Christ becomes at the same time a union with Mary, and this implies the reproduction of her virtues in our lives. Indeed, it is her purity that lives in us when we are pure, her fecund love that is fertile in good works in our own souls when we are zealous in the service of God.

> Let us gain for ourselves the whiteness of her lily-like innocence through our purity of conscience, nor will there be lacking to us the persistence of fruitful work together

with that purity of the flesh which adorned the virginal fruitfulness.* *Ibid.*

Since the whole spiritual life is the life of Christ in us, then Mary, the mother of the Incarnate Word, is the mother of our spiritual life. Our strength in Christ depends on our confidence in Mary. Our confidence in her should be without limits. We should never cease to praise her, no matter how unworthy we may feel. We must constantly give thanks to her for bringing us Jesus. We must seek the mercy of God in and through her. In her we find peace, because in her we find the Truth, the Incarnate Word whom she brings to us. She gives us strong faith and by her intercession defends us against every form of sin. She is the great 'sacrament' of God, so to speak, containing within herself all the abundance of his graces, *charismatum universitas.** *635

Seeking Jesus through Mary is, for Adam, not so much a matter of thinking about Mary and then advancing, by a series of logical steps, to Jesus her Son. It does not mean thinking first about Mary and then about Jesus. It means finding Jesus in and with Mary, Mary in and with Jesus. It means also finding ourselves in them. It means finding that deep spiritual life—the life of God in us—in which we are one with Jesus, in and through the Virgin Mother.

Adam expresses this by saying that we find Jesus and Mary by receiving the life which she has earned for us, by her prayers. We become companions of Jesus,

*636

playing with the Infant Christ at her feet, nourished with him at her breast (*collactanei*)*, embraced with him in her arms. We see Mary exclusively and completely with the eyes of the Infant Christ. We are united to her in him, we are identified with him in her mind, she sees him in us, and us only in him. Hence we must see her as he does also, we must come to her as he did, with his trust and his dependent love. Grace created this love in our hearts.

Our life of dependence on Mary in the order of grace is the simplest and purest expression of our life in Christ.

To seek Christ, therefore, and to seek him through Mary, it is not necessary that we 'rise above' Mary, or somehow exclude her. It is not necessary that we rationalize our relation to Christ and to his blessed mother. It is only necessary that we unite our poverty and helplessness with the Infant Christ, and abandon ourselves to our mother. In this way we find Mary and Jesus together. They are inseparable. But what strikes us first of all is Mary's love and mercy, her mother's love for us. We go on from there to realize more clearly that this is the same love she lavished upon Jesus, and that in this love of hers we are one with him. This love of hers makes us her children by drawing us to her heart with the divine Infant. And it is Christ present in us who makes her love us as her sons.

It is clear to Adam that we do not have to 'climb' or 'ascend' to find Jesus. He has descended to our level in order to give himself completely to us. In his poverty he stands in the midst of us as one whom we know not. To recognize him, we need only love our own nothingness, and see that he has embraced our own poverty for love of us. But if we are devoured by spiritual ambition that resents our own lowliness and seeks to be exalted above our own poverty then we will never find him.

> How delightful it is, how innocent to play together with this infant, to make oneself small to enter his cradle, to speak softly in answer to his infant cries! O how happy is that infancy, which joins its stammering speech with that of such an infant, and wraps itself in his swaddling clothes.*

*635

It is here that Adam goes on to explain that monastic rules and observances are the 'swaddling clothes' with which we are wrapped together with the Infant Christ, by his blessed mother. He takes a very positive view of the restrictions and self-denial of the monastic life—he does not regard them merely as painful and humiliating restraints upon human nature, but above all as means of uniting ourselves with Jesus and plunging ourselves into the love with which he was embraced by Mary.

The love of Our Lady for us does not thereby become an end in itself. The whole organic reality, of Mary's love for us and our union with Jesus her Infant, is the concrete and total expression of God's love for us in the Incarnation. Hence we return to that great central thought: the Incarnation is for Adam not something abstract, but a concrete mystery, which is grasped when we plunge into the very midst of it, when we, too, become infants with the Incarnate Word, and are embraced, with him, by the love of his Virgin Mother.

The Incarnation, then, in its most concrete expression in the life of the monk, is the whole surrounding element of divine love, the new spiritual world in which he lives and moves and is contained, a world made up of Jesus and Mary and of all the souls who are one in Christ enveloped together in the mother-love of Mary, that love in which the mysterious and infinite power of the Spirit works secretly to bring forth new Christs and unite them to the Father.

It is the theme developed in Gerard Manley Hopkins' poem 'The Blessed Virgin Compared to the Air We Breathe':

> *... I say that we are wound*
> *With mercy round and round*
> *As if with air: the same*
> *Is Mary, more by name.*
> *She, wild web, wondrous robe,*
> *Mantles the guilty globe,*
> *Since God has let dispense*
> *Her prayers his providence:*
> *Nay more than almoner,*
> *The sweet alms' self is her*
> *And men are meant to share*
> *Her life as life does air.*
> *If I have understood,*

*She holds high motherhood
Towards all our ghostly good
And plays in grace her part
About man's beating heart,
Laying, like air's fine flood
The deathdance in his blood;
Yet no part but what will
Be Christ our Saviour still.
Of her flesh he took flesh:
He does take fresh and fresh,
Though much the mystery how,
Not flesh but spirit now
And makes, O marvellous!
New Nazareths in us,
Where she shall yet conceive
Him, morning, noon, and eve;
New Bethlehem or Nazareth,
Men here may draw like breath
More Christ and baffle death;
Who, born so, comes to be
New self and nobler me
In each one and each one
More makes, when all is done,
Both God's and Mary's Son....*

*So God was god of old:
A mother came to mould
Those limbs like ours which are
What must make our daystar
Much dearer to mankind;
Whose glory bare would blind
Or less would win man's mind.
Through her we may see him
Made sweeter, not made dim,
And her hand leaves his light
Sifted to suit our sight.*

> *Be thou then, O thou dear*
> *Mother, my atmosphere;*
> *My happier world, wherein*
> *To wend and meet no sin;*
> *Above me, round me lie*
> *Fronting my froward eye*
> *With sweet and scarless sky;*
> *Stir in my ears, speak there*
> *Of God's love, O live air,*
> *Of patience, penance, prayer:*
> *World-mothering air, air wild,*
> *Wound with thee, in thee isled,*
> *Fold home, fast fold thy child.*

THE SABBATH OF CONTEMPLATION

We have now considered in Adam of Perseigne the elements of the monastic life, as it was seen by the Cistercian Fathers, the disciples of St Bernard. We have seen the structural elements of a deep mysticism. There is no room, within these perspectives, for a merely ascetical view of the monastic life. That is to say, there is no place for the idea that the monastic life is simply a collection of observances and 'things to do' which will improve our souls and gain merit for us, so that eventually we will be able to confront Christ as our Judge and receive from him a favorable verdict. Our intimate knowledge of the mystery of Christ is not something reserved only for heaven.

God has already entered deeply into our earthly lives with all the splendors of his wisdom and all the radiance of his eternal joy. The fire of God is playing in our souls, enlivening and transforming them. All our monastic observances are shot through with the flames of this mystical wisdom, and with the transforming power of the Holy Spirit, which is charity. The power of this 'new life'—this *felix novitas*—is ever busy correcting and purifying the traces of sin left in our nature by the 'old man' who has been cast out by our conversion to the monastic life. By his direct action, and through the medium of human agents, particularly the novice master, the Holy Spirit is exorcizing the *spiritus fictionis* in our souls and refashioning our lives according to the pattern of God's own Truth, manifested in Jesus.

Jesus himself is the Master in the school of charity and humility which we have entered, and we have learned that the whole new life, the whole *festivitas* of our new existence in Christ, is simply the concrete expression of the Incarnation, in our own monastic lives. This means that in practice and in the concrete, we can say that Mary is our very life itself, because the new life was brought into the world by her faith and her love, and is kept alive in the world by her constant mediation and her maternal care for all whom she knows and loves in the Infant Christ.

It now remains to round out this brief survey of the Cistercian life by considering that life in its mystical perfection—the 'sabbath' of the soul resting in Christ, and mystically united to him.

The mystical life is the work of the Holy Spirit in the soul of which he has taken full possession by the action of his seven gifts. Here Adam follows the common teaching of the Western Fathers which was later taken up and systematized by St Thomas Aquinas. There is however nothing rigid or systematic about Adam's presentation of the doctrine. The seven gifts, or seven spirits, are simply seven different aspects of that superabundant love of God by which the Holy Spirit celebrates in the soul the mystical festivity of its marriage with the Word.

Adam refers to the gifts as 'seven solemn feasts' or seven holy days, seven sabbaths of rest, 'in which the soul is liberated by God from every servile work in order that it may occupy itself exclusively with him'.* His emphasis, as is usual in the Cistercian Fathers, is upon mystical union as a supreme manifestation of liberty: the liberty of God in choosing the soul for his spouse and the liberty of the soul in responding to the choice. Mystical union is then a feast of supreme freedom, the feast of Truth himself rejoicing in the soul whom he has made free with his own freedom.

Even the gift of fear is, for Adam, a feast of freedom: it is the custodian of the banquet, who dismisses all turbulent and distracting thoughts and enables the soul to feast freely upon divine things.* The fear of the Lord is thus considered not so much as something that makes us attentive

*590

*594

to the danger of sin, but rather as an experience of 'loathing for the labor of making bricks without straw' which Pharaoh (the devil) imposes upon the citizens of 'this world'.

Piety is a feast of sincerity—a feast of truth in God's service, in which love for God's will makes us serve him with joy and self-forgetfulness, and thus drives out of our hearts the 'noise and confusion of evil inclinations'.* Piety, says Adam, 'is worship of God and compassion for the neighbor, a feast in which we taste the beginning of that rest and silence which the prophet called the cult of justice'.* It is also the 'silence in heaven' during which Michael battles with the devil, for in our mystical ascent to God we must face a fierce battle with the spirit of darkness. All the same, this battle does not alter the fact that the soul rests and celebrates in silence the joy of being united with God.

The 'feast of knowledge' illuminates the mind to enable a man to know God and to share his knowledge with others. And so, as we shall see repeatedly, the festivity of silent and solitary union with God by no means excludes good works and fraternal union with others. On the contrary, in proportion as our love of God is purified, so also is our love for our brothers and those are most closely united to their brothers who are at the same time most closely united to God. This is one of the basic principles of Cistercian mysticism and it is strongly emphasized in the letters of

*590

*Cf. Is 32:17

Adam of Perseigne.

In the 'feast of fortitude' we find again the paradoxical union of joy and suffering, peace and combat in the soul united with God. The gift of counsel brings the soul under the direct guidance of Christ 'The Angel of Great Council' but at the same time gives us the ability to direct others in the ways of God's will. The same pattern seems to repeat itself in Adam's descriptions of these various gifts, which shows that his distinctions are not meant to be too clear cut or absolute.

In the 'feast of understanding' the bride of Truth enters into the banquet of the angels. Purified of all images of external things it rejoices in the contemplation of invisible realities that have no bodily image or representation. It is a feast that is 'all splendor' (*tota est splendore*), a feast of spiritual light, and he who is invited to it becomes equal to the cherubim. But he who attains to the 'seventh feast', the feast of Wisdom, reaches the pure and perfect sabbath of charity. This is a feast not of light but of fire. A feast of total transformation, the ultimate goal of the monk's vow of *conversatio morum*. The monk now knows God as perfectly as man in this life can know him—by being consumed in the flames of God's own love. Here he is no longer himself, and yet is most perfectly himself. Having died to himself he finds himself perfectly in God.

One of the most striking things about the mysticism of Adam is the parallel growth of love for God and love for men. The mystic who is transformed by the fire of love in the 'feast of wisdom' is by that very fact brought closer to other men and becomes for them a source of inspiration, drawing them powerfully along the way to the same union. This is done not only by example and teaching, but by a direct communication of the same vehemence of love. The fire of Christ's love leaps from one soul to another, and does so all the more quickly in proportion as they are united in intimate friendship with one another.

Indeed, the Fathers of the Church and the monastic writers of the Middle Ages seldom if ever talk of souls in the abstract and colorless way that we find in a certain type of modern spirituality. There exists today a concept of the apostolate that treats men as objects and numbers rather than as persons. The apostle is regarded almost as if he were an inert instrument, and this instrument is used to 'make converts' in greater or fewer numbers. What seems to matter is not the persons themselves who are converted, their happiness, their growth in Christ, but simply the 'souls' who, without identity and without special features have become eligible for inclusion in statistical estimates of the Church's 'growth'. This is simply an effect of the universal disease of materialism, the worldly reverence for quantity and number. Such things are not so common in the spirituality of earlier centuries.

Although, as we have seen, Adam himself took part enthusiastically in an apostolic movement of vast dimensions, that of Foulques de Neuilly, he seldom speaks of apostolic radiation except in terms of a contact between friends. The communication of love from soul to soul is, for Adam, a communication from friend to friend. When one Christian becomes a saint, his sanctity of course raises the level of sanctity in the whole Church. But what Adam is concerned with is the fact that this sanctity communicates itself to *his immediate circle:* to those with whom he lives, and especially to those with whom he is united by special bonds of friendship. And in this he resembles many of his contemporaries, most of all Aelred of Rievaulx, author of a classic treatise on *Spiritual Friendship.**

*Cistercian Fathers series, number 5 (1974)

The fact that the monk is a 'solitary', and 'flees from the multitude . . . leaving the labors of Martha' for the life of contemplation poses not the slightest problem for Adam. Friendship, and the radiation of spiritual love, is not only no distraction from the contemplation of God, but forms an inseparable part of the contemplative life as he conceives it. Of course, we have to admit that the term 'contemplative life' is itself somewhat alien to Adam. Certainly he seldom uses it in its modern, more or less juridical, sense. For him, it is simply the monastic life, which is a life of love. And wherever there is love, there is sharing of the good gifts which God showers upon

The Feast of Freedom

those who love him. Most of all, there is union and cooperation in the greatest work of all, the work of seeking God and finding him by love. Hence paradoxically love is always at rest, always in silence, always at peace, and yet never idle. *Revera amor numquam est otiosa.** As St Bernard said said somewhere, the very leisure (*otium*) of love is its business (*negotium*). And since the nature of the good is to communicate and share its goodness, love cannot help sharing itself with friends.

*PL 211:596

A good example is the beautiful sixteenth letter, written to one of Adam's close friends, a Benedictine abbot, and through him to his community. Here we have a typical example of that frank, spontaneous and warm affection which is so often found among the medieval and early Christian saints and which seems to have vanished into oblivion in our day, at least in spiritual writing. The thing that is most striking about this open expression of deep spiritual friendship is its patently eucharistic character. Indeed it is obvious that such friendship should exist as the normal fruit of our participation in the eucharistic banquet.

> Let us love Christ and in Him let us love one another for nothing is happier in this life than to love faithfully and to be loved.* Break your bread [says Adam] break your bread to your begging and hungry friend; for in this you will prove yourself a friend if you will

*640

allay your friend's hunger with your bread. Your bread is Christ. Your bread is your love. Your bread is your prayer. Your bread is your compunction of tears with which you wash away not only your own sins but also those of your friend.*

*594

An exclamation in a letter to his Benedictine friend sums it all up: 'All that I have to write to you is about love'. *Tota mihi tecum est de amore materies.**

*632

Never for a moment does Adam consider that this friendship in Christ is a distraction or a disturbance to his life of prayer. But how is this possible? Only because his love itself is so eminently simple, strong and pure. It is completely free from worldliness, from falsity, from the *spiritus fictionis* which seeks its own selfish satisfaction under the cover of lofty spirituality. Here is no disguise, no pretense, no hidden selfishness. Certainly there is satisfaction and joy. But they are pure, and the love of his friends has become, in all truth, one and the same thing with his love for Christ.

In one word, this true love is not and cannot be unhealthy because it is the fruit of his union with Christ. Christ is the head of the mystical body, says Adam, and a love that is ruled by Christ the head of the body must inevitably be normal and healthy and free. It is perfectly 'sane'. But worldly love only gets into us by separating us from Christ our head. Such love then, does not come from our 'head' and therefore it is an 'insanity'.*   *640

This then sums it all up. Love is the answer to everything for Adam as it was for St John and for Christ Himself. 'God is charity, and he who remains in charity remains in God and God in him'.*   *I John 4:16

This love is the soul's bond with God as the source of all reality, and therefore such love is itself the triumph of truth in our lives. Hence it drives out all falsity all error. To remain in love is to remain in the truth. All that one has to do is to continue loving, in sincerity and truth, and seeking before all else the will of God. Everything else follows. Life is then a perpetual 'sabbath' of divine peace.

When the soul of the monk has arrived at perfect union with the will of Christ, so that there is no longer any discrepancy between them, the light of holy fear and compunction no longer discover anything to reproach, and the soul tastes perfect peace and contentment. It rests in the interior silence of a pure heart in which Christ is present. The soul is perfectly tranquil because it is in harmony with the supreme Truth of God himself, in Christ.

> Peace prepares a chamber of rest for a man in the testimony his conscience gives him, to whom justice more sweetly offers its kiss, the more it takes away every wound of sin by the proposal of truth.*   *PL 211:620

Humility, meekness, and obedience have played the most important part in producing this interior peace. How? By bringing the soul into complete dependence on Christ, and total freedom from every other influence.* Liberated from all cares, because free from every other desire than the desire of pleasing Christ, the soul is delivered from the tyranny of sensual attractions and from all interest in the things of the world. It tastes already the joys of eternity in the 'sabbath of innocence'.

*See Ep 18; PL 211:645

Within there takes place the sabbath of innocence keeping festival in days of eternal peace.*

*Ibid.

The light of perfect charity has risen in the pure heart, the orient star which brings us, like the Magi, to the true King.* This is the star of peace, the star of love, whose rays are the splendor of the divine festival in the depths of our soul. Under the rays of this star, the soul enters the *cella vinaria* and tastes the sweetness of contemplation. Now the monk no longer knows the labor of learning or the toil of discipline. The soul rests in the arms of the Spouse, and sings the nuptial song of union with Him Who alone is her glory and her joy.* This is the full and perfect flowering of the monastic life.

*Ep 16; 637

*Ep 18; 648

Thomas Merton

THE LETTERS OF *ADAM of PERSEIGNE*

LETTER I
TO
WILLIAM, BISHOP OF ELY *

*William Longchamp, Bishop of Ely 1189–1197.

LETTER I

1

WILLIAM, BISHOP OF ELY and Chancellor of the Lord King of England, greeting in the spirit of truth from Brother Adam. It is partly your intimacy which we undeservedly enjoy and partly our necessity by which we are weighed down that make us by your frequent letters or messages wearisome to your highness. Nevertheless, with generous spirits neither of them is taken amiss, because the sincerity of a happy friendship prevents friendliness from becoming lack of respect and sympathy is not withheld when pity is needed. Therefore emboldened on both counts I am not afraid to bring before your eyes a letter even lengthier than usual, although your preoccupation with affairs so diverse, so numerous, may keep them from reading it—a preoccupation which does not allow you even an hour's respite.

2. In the midst of a catastrophe so great and so widespread, to possess a friend is to have lost him, because when danger is everywhere threatening virtue,

scarcely any virtue can survive, and this alone it is that we love in our friends. Where that has without doubt perished, we cease to have a friend, and the virtue that, if preserved, could produce joy over the friend, when lost engenders sorrow and grief. Happy the love whose only root is virtue and praiseworthy that friendship which, having no other source than virtue of the spirit, asks for itself no other stimulus. It is in this and for this that we cherish your venerable self. May the flood of worldly vanity in whose whirlpool you are so dangerously swimming not grudge us this good in our friend. Truly I shall call you friend as long as virtue of soul exists in you, so that you either preserve it with careful determination or speedily hasten to restore it if it has collapsed.

3. How difficult it is for one walking in a slippery place not to totter frequently or fall headlong. How hard it is for one walking in darkness not to stumble often, fall heavily, be grievously battered. When the wind blows this way and that one rarely walks uncertainly along the edge of a precipice without being thrust violently from the heights to the depths. Easily do such things befall those whom love of virtue does not support nor love of truth enlighten. When these two qualities are lacking the situation is dangerous and for such a man life is nothing but an abyss. I say abyss—it is a land whose whole surface is wrapped in darkness, where knowledge of the truth is unsupported by zeal for

virtue. How happy the soul which does not despise the possession of such treasures, the soul which the desire for them draws to the heights and which does not allow itself to become involved in the foulness of things low and vile. For the soul is of such nobility that its nature is to seek what is higher, if however it is not led astray by its own judgement. To secure this, the brightness of virtue is of service, for when it has drawn away the clouds of error from the sky of pure reason it weighs sincerely and values the truth that flashes upon it. Thereafter by no means will that brightness so auspiciously flashing become worthless in the eyes of the soul that sets a right value on itself. But in it, midday as it were, succeeds the morn when from the sight and experience of the brightness it blazes forth into love's desire. Thereupon love of virtue is joined to splendor of truth and in the mind that one day is rejoicing the day known to the Lord, the day of gladness, the festal day sprung from him. This is the day which the Lord has made,* the day of exultation and gladness whose joyful rays the unhappy sons of darkness are not worthy to enjoy. 'Sons of darkness' we call those who do not go forth from the underground of the wretched flesh, who in the prison-houses of their bodies, slaves to the works of darkness, remain for ever nowhere but in the tombs of conscience. O wretched thraldom, to be bewailed with a whole fount of tears, to deem as delight a servitude to thorns, to believe the forward

*Ps 118:24

Letter I

march of malice and its freedom from punishment to be glory, to set the licence to sin before the freedom of righteousness. How far are such things from the sons of light, from the citizens of heaven, from the followers of the Crucified! Of a truth, the Israelites do not stay in Egypt nor strive after the slavish works of mud and brick.* Neither the crossing of the Red Sea** nor the unfamiliar bitterness of loneliness hinders them from seeking after the delights of the promised sweetness.

*Cf. Ex 1:14
**Cf. Ex 14: 19-31

5. What shall we say of Moses, Israel's leader? Not only does he loathe submission to Pharaoh but by his eager advocacy stirs his people to pant after the land flowing with milk and honey.* It is unseemly for a leader of the nation, a guardian of the church to be subservient to the train of an earthly king. Instead he must go forth from Egypt and tread the path which Israel follows when returning to his native land. It is fitting that he who bears the cross of Christ as the leader in the march, should go forth at the head of the procession and by his example rouse those who follow to bear whatever cross there be for the attaining of salvation.

*Ex 3:17, 13:5, 33:3

6. What unhappy times are ours! How pitiful the habits of mankind! How deserving of tears those especially whom we should have had as our defenders! The leaders of the nation have forgotten the land of promise and, lured by the sweetness of voluptuous slavery, they have brought themselves and their people under

the domination of Pharaoh, from which there is little escape. Would that this slavery to Egypt prove displeasing to you in the face of your desire for true liberty and that you love with courage that of which you have acquired the knowledge does not allow you to be ignorant. For you need a stout heart and on a foundation of manly virtue not to live a woman in Egypt where it was decreed by Pharaoh that the males be strangled.* Happier it is to live with the virtues than to drift womanish into the softness of vice when the dread limit of a spurious sweetness changes into absinthe of an eternal bitterness. This your discretion knows full well, and, if the world which lays its commands upon you were to allow you to ponder such matters, you would have fuller knowledge and a more effective eloquence.

*Ex 1:15-16

7. Do someday what you know should be done and what you seem to approve and praise in those who do it. If in your eyes they are commendable whom uprightness of life makes praiseworthy, it is commendable also that you share with those you consider worthy of approval the fellowship of their virtuous life. If the court of a mortal king, weighed down with anxieties, is an obstacle to you, reflect rather on the care demanded by your office, in which you must take such thought for the sheep entrusted to your protection. For the rest, Father, as we sincerely desire for you what is good, so we are praying unceasingly for you. May nothing so stand in the way of

our prayers as to deprive them of their effectiveness.

8. We earnestly commend to your generosity the bearer of these presents, whom at your behest we have agreed to send over to England. May your care on his behalf secure that the toil involved in such a journey, especially since it has been undertaken at your direction, shall not be to the lessening of your glory and injury to our brotherly affection, or remain without the profit we have looked for. Farewell.

LETTER II
TO
MASTER ANDREW

his friend, Canon of Tours,*
from brother Adam,
charity from a pure heart.

*Perhaps Archdeacon Andrew of Tours. See
Ceillier, Histoire générale des Auteurs sacrés,
14:881.

LETTER II
9

I WAS INDEED PREPARING to obey your command, dear one, but feeling myself quite unequal to carrying out your order, I am almost going back on my undertaking. My slender ability does not correspond to the lofty subject which you set me and my conscience, seared by the branding iron of sin, does not presume to speak without anxiety of the glorious praises of the glorious Mother of God. For into my soul, turning toward the depths through the weight of its earthly inclination, is struck terror by a kind of majestic glory which I at all times reflect on in the excellent Mother of God—though with defective vision. She, now saluted by the angel*, now made fruitful by the Holy Spirit†, now raised to the height of all the virtues, honored by the leaping of the yet-unborn Jesus, commended by the prophetic words of Elizabeth*, cries out and says: 'my soul magnifies the Lord'.* Therefore I greatly fear lest the Mother of God, most worthy of all praise, should consider as a lessening of her praise whatever I can

*Lk 1:28
†Lk 1:35

*Lk 1:41-5
*Lk 1:46-55

stammer forth with lips uncircumcised, especially since unlovely is praise in a sinner's mouth*. But because I abide by my promise and am supported by the approval of your charity, I betake myself to the fragrant chamber, to the storehouse of wisdom, to Mary, mother of pity, so that she whose soul magnifies the Lord may not shrink from being magnified, that is, extolled by my mouth. *Si 15:9*

10. Mary says: 'my soul magnifies the Lord.'* Note first where she magnifies the Lord. Surely in the mountains of Judaea, in the house of Zachariah. The Lord is magnified in the mountains; he is blasphemed on the plains. On the plains were those who, according to the prophet, blasphemed holy Israel and were turned again into strangers.* On the plains, I say, of the curse and shame of Adam and Eve who after losing the integrity of the flesh, aliens from the heights of truth, made for themselves aprons.* For they had lost the mountain heights of truth and virtue. Therefore from the vale of worldly vanity, from the depth of man's corruption, from the plains of general injustice, Mary arose and went with haste to the mountains.* The mountains are pinnacles of perfection. The pinnacles themselves are the truth of a fully illumined mind, the virginity of unstained flesh, the virtue of the highest overshadowing her, to make pregnant her womb. These are the mountains to which Mary ascends. This is the city of Judah, this the house of Zachariah.

Lk 1:46

Is 1:4

Gn 3:7

Lk 1:39

11. A city is a great assembly of men living under a common law. This people is made by the reasoned considerations of Mary, her holy virtues, her disciplined actions which the law of charity disposes in her proclamation of God's praise. Indeed Judah means 'proclamation'; Zachariah, 'mindful of \God'. The house of Zachariah is the virgin heart which is mindful of God's commands.

12. Among these mountains was set the Mother of God and while, as Elizabeth prophesies, she hears what one shall be, while she recalls what she heard by the angel's message concerning the Lord, while she reflects on the purity of her conscience, while she considers her flesh kept free from all corruption, while she sees her whole being brought to the highest point by God's action, already exalted above the world, already far above every creature by the merit of her life, by the privilege of unique grace, by the greatness of her joy, she sings a new song to the Lord, saying: 'my soul magnifies the Lord'.

13. The soul of Mary magnifies the Lord because she herself is magnified by the Lord. For unless she were first magnified by the Lord, Mary's soul could not magnify the Lord. Therefore she magnifies him by whom she is magnified, magnifies him not only by the speech of her lips, not only by the holiness of her body, but by the unequaled quality of her love. Many magnify him with their tongue but blaspheme him with their deeds and

become persecutors through the arrogance of their hearts. Of them it is written: 'They confess that they know God but deny him by their deeds'.* They do not magnify him, but as much as in them lies they belittle the name of the Lord. These are they to whom the apostle says: 'Through you my good name is blasphemed among the nations.'*

*Tt 1:16

*Rm 2:24

14. But in Mary her tongue, her life, her soul, all magnify the Lord—her tongue by proclaiming the magnificence of holiness in praise of the divine glory, her soul by its unique love, by achieving it on the wings of contemplation, by grasping with mind and heart his unfathomable magnificence. 'My soul,' she says, 'magnifies the Lord.'

15. How do you magnify him? Do you make greater him whose magnificence has no end? Great is the Lord, says the Psalmist, and greatly to be praised.* Great he is, and so great that his greatness has neither comparison nor measure. How then do you magnify one whom you cannot from small make great nor from great greater? But you magnify because you praise, you magnify because amid the darkness of the world, being brighter than the sun, lovelier than the moon, more fragrant than the rose, whiter than snow, you spread abroad the splendor of the knowledge of God. You magnify him therefore not by increasing his surpassing greatness but by bringing the unknown radiance of the true deity to the world's darkness. For the Lord

*Ps 145:3

whom you magnify, since he is eternal, knows no failure and, since he is perfect, knows no increase. He is eternal for he has neither beginning nor end. He is perfect for his fulness nothing is lacking. But him you magnify when you so far raise yourself by your surpassing merits that you receive the fulness of grace [and] merit the coming upon you of the Holy Spirit, [and] that, being made the Mother of God, remaining still a pure virgin, you bring forth for the perishing world a Saviour. But for what reason? Because the Lord is with you and he has made your merits his gift. Therefore the more you are magnified in him and by him, the more you are said to magnify him. What then does your 'soul magnifies the Lord' mean but this: that you are so magnified by him that you gain magnificently the fulness of grace and, by your virtues glorious and surpassing all others, you reach out to the magnificence of a unique glory. You reach out, I say, because you are drenched with all the dew of the Holy Spirit, you are inundated wholly with heavenly unction, so that after the fashion of a skin that is anointed your soul stretches so far through its longing for love that it reaches the very word of God. For you are Moses' basket*, you are the vessel containing the Word, you are the storehouse of the new wine by which the soberness of believers becomes inebriated. You are the Mother of God, the limit set to sin, by whom men rise from the depths of vice and reach the delights of angels.

*Cf. Ex 2:3

16. How your works are magnified*, our Lady! But it is through him whom your soul magnifies. Here indeed my insignificance, striving to speak of your magnificance, utterly fails. For while you go up into the mountains of the magnificance of virtues, so that there you may magnify the Lord, I, unhappy wretch, am plunged into the depths of misery and vice. But you, mother of mercy, because I am a kind of stone in the heap of Mercury, because I am lead in swirling water*, because I am weighed down, because I cannot move, draw me after you that I may be strong enough to run in the odor of your perfumes,* breathe in the examples of your virtues, be aided by the wings of your discourses, so that at your petition, my soul may first learn by fearing God to withdraw from evil and afterwards, with you, by loving and doing justice may learn to magnify the Lord, to whom is honour and glory and might and power for ever and ever.

*Cf. Ps 104:24

*Ex 15:10

*Sg 1:3-4

LETTER III
TO
THE VENERABLE ABBOT

of Turpenay,*
his father and dear friend in Christ,
Brother Adam, sinner,
sends greeting in the Holy Spirit.

*William, abbot of Turpenay, 1142-88(?), a Benedictine monastery in the forest of Chinon, diocese of Tours.

LETTER III

17

THE HOLY LOVE, which has closely bound us with a mutual knitting of our minds, delays no longer to pay that which it did not fail to promise. You well recall, dear friend, I think you have not forgotten, what was promised you at your earnest request. Surely your affection, which rejoiced so greatly in the promise, has not allowed the pleasure of anticipation to be suspended or you to forget it. But what reason for rejoicing do you expect from me but faithful love in return and happy experience of it? For you indeed there will be a certain kind of experience—the love of a letter more affectionate if it proceeds from a sweet friendship. Discover by experience in my letters the warmth of my affection. Although friendship is usually valued more surely as a result of the performance of actions and their witness, yet in this the power of love is the object, and you are seeking nothing from my love but that through it my whole being might pass into you.

18. The holiness of a chaste love with-

drawing into the very depths of the heart holds in suspicion everything outside it, and considers nothing to be safer than that, with conscience as its witness, it remain hidden. Happy the love whose enemy is worldly hope. Caring nothing for the anxieties of the fleeting world, it does not derive its sustenance from the pleasures of the flesh. It derives its incentive from another source, concerned to gain heavenly things, not unmindful of contempt for earthly affairs, impatient of everything unseemly, but ungrateful for benefits received. Holy love therefore has its seed plot in the virtue of the soul; its foundation and subsequent course lie in its longing for truth undefiled.

19. Love it is that is the entire topic between us, but it concerns that love for which virtue is the foundation, truth its study, purity its desire, piety its work, instruction in discipline its way of life. Nothing is sweeter than love and, since it has no value apart from itself, it is also its own reward. The word love is common to things that are very different, but all ambiguity is removed because of what has already been said. But if we wish to give it its proper name, it is called in Scripture affection or charity. The difference is that the word 'love' has more the sound of a natural faculty but the word 'charity' expresses the influence of grace.

20. Among the powers of the soul none is more worthy than love, none sweeter, none equally strong. It is shameful that the

best thing we have should turn into the desire for something of less worth. Let love either delight in itself or if it is not sufficient for itself let it seek a more fortunate joy in heavenly things. In heavenly things there is a joy obtained from reverence and love of the supreme good—when it is cultivated with piety and zeal. This sole and supreme good, as it is sought by love alone and by love alone is attained, so also, once attained, by love alone is kept. Love seeks it, love finds it; love holds and keeps it and does not let it go. 'I have held him' it says 'and will not let him go.'* For love seeks with tenderness, finds with gladness, enjoys with blessedness and is fulfilled. It does not seek without light nor find without sweetness. It does not enjoy without fulness and it does not end. This which is counted the supreme good, possessing nothing beyond itself, has nothing beneath itself to satisfy itself.

*Sg 3:4

21. The supreme good is indeed God himself, supreme because self-deriving, self-sufficient, living all-powerful, possessing all wisdom of unfailing goodness. He is of unconquered might which has brought the universe into existence. He is of purest wisdom which has brought order and beauty into creation; of unsullied goodness which has divided to each created thing a degree of usefulness in accordance with his good pleasure. Learning to know this good makes you good; loving it makes you happy; persevering in it will make you blessed from your enjoyment of it.

22. But to the splendor of such grace, to the delight of such glory the spirit advances by certain steps and, advancing, soars to the heights. And the first step is to abstain utterly from all that is unlawful. The second is that, if you so despise things unlawful, they do not enter into your desire. The third is to disdain, as far as necessity allows, even things that are lawful. The fourth is a constant and eager observance of the commandments. The fifth is a careful and constant watchfulness of soul to guard your purity. The sixth is a striving after the virtues and a hunger for spiritual progress. The seventh is, even among the very virtues. to strive after the higher gifts. The eighth is a humble and devout giving of thanks and the uttering of praise when the gifts have been received. The ninth is, when compared with the longing for the supreme good, no visible thing passes into the affections. The tenth is the correction of the memory and the expulsion of physical imagination so that the insolence of Bilhah may not cheat the sweetness of the longed-for Rachel.* Often it happens to the contemplative that when he longs for Rachel's beauty—that is, the purity of contemplation—Bilhah, Rachel's hand maid—that is, the physical imagination—forces herself violently upon Jacob's desires. For the rest, in the end Jacob embraces Rachel, and Ahasuerus, fainting for love, weds the beautiful Esther.* Truly when this ladder has been climbed, the soul has reached the consummation of an

*Cf. Gn 29:29-30:9

*Cf. Est 2:17

unstained purity insofar as mortal nature allows and the experience of a marvellous sweetness melts it. Being melted, it cries out and says: 'My soul faints for your salvation and in your word have I hoped.'* It pours forth the remembrance of the sweetness it has experienced* and praises it. It marvels and cries out, saying: 'How great is the abundance of your sweetness, O Lord, which you have kept secret for those who fear you'.*

*Ps 119:81

*Cf. Ps 145:7

*Ps 31:19

23. I beseech you, dearest, if by the prompting of the Holy Spirit you one day reach this place, do not lay aside amid such delights the remembrance of your friend.* Remember me, I say, when it shall be well with you and though you dare not bring in one who lacks the marriage garment,* do not be ashamed to beg on your friend's behalf pardon for his sins. For I am the unhappiest of men, for though I dare rashly to speak of such matters, I do not deserve as yet to have reached even the first step. For I dwell wholly among things unlawful and, since I have so often done what is unlawful, I have not deserved to have the lawful allowed me. How do I dare to direct my speech toward heaven and discourse upon the nature and glory of the supreme good when the heap of my misfortunes crushes me and almost renders me destitute of goodness? What has a wretched man to do with a discussion of goodness? What has one full of faults to do with a discourse on virtues? What has one who is collapsing to do with pointing out things

*Gn 40:14

*Cf. Mt 22:11-14

that are above? Alas, with what shame does one who is wretched, dying, poor despicable, lying in the filth of his offenses, speak and discourse upon sanctity? With a new type of presumption a fool philosophizes on the study of wisdom and an ignoramus feels no embarrassment in teaching what he never learned. I have indeed become a fool but your love has constrained me,* as well as my own promise to which I was held. If I have gone too far, because on weighty and wonderful subjects my poverty and insignificance have advanced above themselves,* forgive me. Henceforth I must employ a moderate tone and let my speech be rather about what concerns the healing of wounds.

*2 Co 12:11

*Cf. Ps 131:1

24. Therefore since the splendor of heavenly things is painful to eyes that are weak, let us turn our bleary eyes to the pillar of cloud and darkness.* Truly the pillar of cloud and darkness is the fixed sublimity of our Virgin from which the brightness of the godhead has drawn over itself a kind of darkness. For while the splendor of the omnipotent Word, through the conception of the Virgin, was wrapped in the cloud of flesh, what was the likeness of sin in that flesh but a kind of darkness in a cloud. Clouds, it says, and darkness surround it* because the splendor of the Word was covered over with a cloud of purest flesh and in the same flesh surrounded with weakness. But let us turn our thoughts to that pillar of which we previously spoke.

*Cf. Ex 13:21; Nm 12:5

*Ps 97:2

25. Let us note how stout, how straight, how upright it is. Let us note, I say, how strong, how straight, how smooth, how long, how lofty it is. How stout it is on which heaven and earth lean. How strong is that which battles invincibly against all heresies and spiritual wickedness. How smooth, which admits no wrinkle of deceit. How lofty, which surpasses every creature by the height of its merits. How raised on high, whom the Son of the Most High foresaw from eternity as his most worthy mother. How happy is she who is both mother and spouse of God, the gate of heaven, the loveliness of paradise, lady of angels, queen of the universe, joy of the saints, advocate of believers, courage of those who fight, the recaller of those who wander, medicine of the penitent. O sure salvation! Short path to life! Sole hope of pardon, sweetness unique. You, Lady, are my all. In your hands has been stored for me the fulness of all good. With you have been hidden the unfailing treasures of truth and grace, of peace and pity, of salvation and wisdom, of glory and of honor. You are my anchor amid the billows, port in shipwreck, support in tribulation, comfort in grief. You are, for those who are yours, aid in oppression, help in time of crisis, temperance in prosperity, joy in time of waiting, refreshment in toil. Whatsoever I can stammer in your praise is less than your praise, for you are worthy of all praise. Yet am I bound to praise you.

26. If I speak with the tongue of men

Letter III

and of angels* when I have poured out my whole self, it will be too little. I have recourse rather to that praise of you which is sung thus in the song of love: 'Who is she who goes forth as the rising dawn, beautiful as the moon, glorious as the sun, terrible as an army in array?'* With these words, briefly and simply, truthfully and loftily, is expressed the fourfold praise of your glory. For when you are born, you arise like the glowing dawn. Truly your rising took the office of dawn for in it the day of grace began. The night of infidelity and ignorance was ended. When you conceive the sun of righteousness, you like the moon are illumined by the good office of the blazing sun. The moon borrows from the sun the light which the nature of its gross body denies it. Therefore whatever beauty it possesses it has through the gift of its borrowed splendor. When you bring forth the sun of righteousness, you are compared to the sun because of the close likeness. Just as the body of the sun is not injured or diminished when it puts forth its rays, so the bringing forth of the holy birth does not violate the mother.* And what, you who are glorious as the sun, what is your offspring but the eternal splendor of a certain sun? This splendor shines everywhere, even in the darkness and yet the darkness is not worthy to grasp it. Finally this splendor enlightens every man coming into this world.* But men have loved darkness more than light.* But to you, mother of pity, the choice of the

*Cf. 1 Co 13:1

*Sg 6:9

*Cf. Bernard, Miss 2:17; PL 183:70c

*Cf. Jn 1:5,9
*Cf. Jn 3:19

sun is fitting for you reveal to all men the rays of eternal splendor.

27. Moreover, when you were taken up into the heavens from the evil world you were made terrible as an army in battle array to every spiritual wickedness. Therefore you were at the dawn at its rising, you possessed the beauty of the full moon while becoming full of grace* by the conception of the word made flesh. Rightly have you been compared to the sun, remaining without spot in childbirth, terrible as an army in array, in your passing-over at which amid heavens' rejoicing, the angels reverencing, the saints exulting, and the banners of virtue waving, you have appeared a terror to demons.

*Lk 1:28

28. Therefore, dear friend, all our confidence lies in the childbearing of our Virgin and though I may be unworthy I shall not cease to dwell upon her praises. If you stand in need of mercy, it is found in full measure in the heart of the Virgin. If you reverence the truth, give thanks to the Virgin, since from the ground of her virgin flesh the truth which you worship has arisen.* No less give thanks to the Virgin if you follow after peace, since from her is born for you the peace which passes all understanding.* If you pursue justice, see that you are not ungrateful to the Virgin, for at the opening of her womb justice looked forth from heaven.* If your faith is shaken by some assault from an enemy, turn your eyes upon the Virgin and that in which was wavering will be firmly fixed. If

*Cf. Ps 85:12

*Cf. Ph 4:7

*Cf. Ps 85:11, 1 Co 1:30

the lust of the flesh delights you, turn your gaze upon the Virgin, and the danger to your chastity is removed. If pride disturbs your spirit, turn your gaze upon the Virgin, and by the merit of her unsullied humility your swelling spirit will subside. If you are set on fire by anger's torches, lift your eyes to the Virgin and you will grow gentle through her calm. If ignorance or error have led you astray from the way of life, look to Mary, star of the sea, and in her light you will be led back to the path of truth. If the vice of avarice commands your idolatrous worship, call to mind the generosity of the Virgin and with a love of poverty there will come to you the goodness of openhandedness. In every peril the goodness of the Virgin comes to succour, and powerful is it to succour. Give thanks for her childbearing; from her fulness the sum total of graces has flowed. For us the Virgin brought forth, ours is the birth, for us the child was born and to us the son was given.*

*Is 9:6

29. How delightful and blameless it is to play with the little child, to be close to his cradle, to share in his crying. How happy that infancy which lisps along with such a babe and wraps itself in his swaddling bands. Surely by the clothes in which the infant Word is wrapped the filth of evil deeds is wiped away; by the crying of the little one are balanced the everlasting wailings which those who scoff at innocence have deserved. The swaddling band with which he is pressed in his cradle is the bond

of holy religion. The straw in which he lay, which he kept beneath him, points to the flesh which subjects itself to the spirit. He was laid in a manger.* What do we mean by that but that the food of our souls has been laid on the altar? For the manger represents that altar which feeds holy beings with the sacred body of Christ. These are the things by which the love of God is shown to us. These are the things by which our love is kindled and fed. Dwelling on them produces fear, moves us to goodness, instructs us in the way of knowledge, strengthens us to endure, spurs us on to counsel, enlightens us to understanding, fires us to wisdom, prepares us for our crown. The all-powerful Word straitened itself to become a tiny child so that as an infant he might be like infants and being humble might fit himself to the humble.*

*Cf. Lk 2:7

*Verbum omnipotens se abbreviavit. Cf. Rm 9:28, Bernard, V Nat 1.1; OB 4:197.

30. Meanwhile, let all our philosophy be concerned with the infancy of the Word incarnate and let us who in some measure estimate from it God's love for us be eager to reflect upon it with all our might and with sincerity. I dare not say 'the same measure' because just as there is no counting of his bounty and wisdom, so his love is immeasurable and eternal. And he who is in essence love entire, for whom to love is simply to be, loves himself completely. How differently they love—love and lover, the one who is moved and the mover, he who is love and he who is a sharer in the love. Deity poured itself wholly into man, the soul offered itself wholly to obedience,

the body delivered itself wholly to death, even death on a cross.* Thus the omnipotent loved us utterly and it is too small a thing if we pay in return all our modest means all that we are. We did not will to die for him and he himself would rather die for us than fail in his love for us.

*Ph 2:8

31. But it is too soon to treat of the death of the child by whose cradle we lately frolicked, playing with his happy childhood. I pray you, let us still return to the cradle, still be as children with the child, taking the food of our childhood from his tiny mouthfuls. Let us join him as he sucks the breast, if perchance some drop from that sweetest milk may fall upon us. Believe me, he does not grudge his mother's breast to those who share her milk with him, he grants them a place so that they may stay between her breasts. Those breasts are full of heaven,* they strengthen by their unfailing sweetness and are never without a throng who suck them. And the compassionate mother herself is wont not to deny herself to those who suck, though she keeps her whole self for her only Son. O unfailing fulness! Abundance of sweetness which the thirst of babes sucks from the breasts of the tender Virgin. If you will, it is good for us to be here,* it is good to abide here longer, nowhere can we be better than here. Wonderful is this new thing known only to little ones, that Wisdom, the nurse of angels, should need to be nourished with the Virgin's milk. What wonder if our infancy's poverty

*Cf. Antiphon Nesciens Mater for Vespers within the Octave of Christmas in the Cistercian breviary.

*Mt 17:4, Mk 9:5, Lk 9:33

should long for the sustenance of this milk, since by that milk the strength and wisdom of God boast that they are strengthened. Indeed by that same mother's milk is our hunger fed if the flames of hell are extinguished by the tiny tears of a crying child. Even so, as we express the joy of our hearts in great solemnities, let us hear from the shepherds themselves what news they bring of the splendors of a sun new-rising. To our Sun neither the witness of the shepherds nor the proclamation of angels is lacking. Your testimonies, O Lord, have been made clear.* Wonderful are your testimonies O Lord, therefore has my soul searched them out.* What can be held more sacred, what perceived with greater sweetness, what believed with greater profit? What heard with greater gain, what thought in loftier terms, what preached with greater truth?

*Ps 93:5

*Ps 119:129

32. Truly, well do we spend pleasant days of ease at such a heartfelt festival. Yet the harshness of the eighth day, close at hand, makes us shudder and not without reason clouds over the brightness of our festival, for the severity of circumcision brings martyrdom to the delicacy of the unspotted flesh. Who would even hear without pity that the tender flesh was harshly cut—that flesh which, wholly ignorant of guilt, came to put an end to sin. Rightly do we attack the law which deems a lamb of perfect innocence in need of its remedies. Too cruel is the circumcision which is practised in the letter and not the

spirit, which cuts into the flesh and not into the fault. Let us pass rather to that circumcision which is of the heart. Yet, I pray you, let the child be circumcised, let the lawgiver be subject to the law's control. Let him receive what he himself gave that the law may finish where it began. The law of Christ is the truth of love which circumcises every fault. The law is love for it binds and restrains and while it destroys everything that is evil it can itself never fail. For charity never fails;* this love unites us. This love holds festival in hearts that do not leave Christ's cradle.

*1 Co 13:8

33. In the Magi this love visits the child and worships him with the mysteries of the three gifts. See, meanwhile, our festival has shone forth and the star of faith, more resplendent than the world's rising sun has led us to the true orient. I mispoke in saying 'has led', unless perchance something would have led us away from him. It is better to linger in his presence; nowhere else is salvation, nowhere is safety without him. Let us always cling to what is ours, let our festival be extended to the joys of Simeon,* Let his mother not offer him without us. Let his solemn presentation find us present in the temple. Would that a like pure love might make us the pair of turtle doves in that offering. Would that the simplicity of holy charity might reveal us as a pair of dove fledglings. For by these virtues, by these figurative birds we shall be able to redeem for ourselves our Redeemer. Not yet is this the offering of

*Lk 2:25-35

himself to death, not yet is the passion suited to the time or age. By our love of chastity, by our longing for simplicity, if neither lacks the twofold charity,* we are able to keep Jesus with us.

*of God and neighbor. Cf. Mt 22:37-40

34. Let Jesus be nourished among us, among us let him advance in years and wisdom* that at the fitting moment he may be ready for his passion. Meanwhile he is little, he does not think of the passion, instead he must be busy with the breast. But if he has fled to avoid Herod's swords, let Egypt receive him without us.* It is more blessed to remain with him in a hiding place than to spend one's time and strength venturing on great exploits before men's eyes. If he has wished or his mother has counselled us to stay near the swords, it is right to suffer death on behalf of innocence. When he returns from Egypt, let us live with him at Nazareth that we may be able to give forth sweet fragrance from the blossoms of a life in its springtime. For Nazareth is called a flower and it is appropriate that he should blossom forth in virtue who is wont to offer the Virgin's son a friendly lodging. If at twelve years old, without his parents' knowledge, he willed to remain in Jerusalem, happy are we if he willed us to be sharers in his action. O happy three days! Feast of pure joy—for all those three days to be free to attend to him, to direct one's thoughts to him, to be refreshed by the words of grace which proceed from his mouth!* It is not seemly for him to be sought elsewhere, he will

*Cf. Lk 2:52

*Cf. Mt 2

*Lk 2:41-52, Cf. Aelred, Iesu; Cf. 2

always be occupied in his Father's business,* and would that we were never separated from him. If he drew near to the river Jordan to be baptized of John,* it behoves us to follow thither the very fount of life, we who need to be washed by him for so many grievous faults. Being washed by him, we shall advance in Christ in manifold ways so that, through the opening of the heavens, the witness of the Father's voice, the descent of the Holy Spirit as a dove, the salutation of John himself, we may love more perfectly him whom we have recognized.*

*Cf. Lk 2:49

*Mt 3:13.
Cf. Mk 1:9,
Lk 3:21

*Mt 3:11-17,
Mk 1:7-11,
Lk 3:16,
Gn 1:26-36

35. Thus far have we followed Jesus. How, after this, shall we desert him, either when he was led by the Spirit into the wilderness or when tempted by the devil?* Otherwise with what impudence shall we dare to be present at the marriage or approve the changing of tasteless water into wine?* Or how shall we be able to share in the joys of the marriage if we are unwilling to share in his afflictions? 'You,' says the Lord, 'are they who have continued with me in my afflictions, and I appoint for you a kingdom, as my Father has appointed me.'* How happy is the willing endurance of temptation, by which the appointment to a heavenly kingdom is prepared. But for the strengthening of faith, for the increase of hope, for the stirring up of love, it is essential that he who grew strong by reason of the innocence of the infant should now attain to a perfect man by reason of the youth's

*Mt 4:1-11,
Mk 1:12-13,
Lk 4:1-13

*Jn 2:1-11

*Lk 22:28-29

strength. Now the child has grown into the youth, speaking wonderful words, doing marvellous deeds. Now he is curing paralytics, cleansing lepers, giving sight to the blind, hearing to the deaf, steps to the lame, speech to the dumb. He raises the dead, puts demons to flight, commands the winds and the sea, cures every infirmity by the word of command alone;* out of his pity receives sinners, understands the thoughts of men's hearts, refreshes five thousand men with five loaves, confounds the pride of Pharisees and the wisdom of scribes by his wondrous answer to every word.* More marvellous than all this, he strives to show to every injury an all-embracing patience, and although with his complete innocence he possesses complete power, still he preserves complete obedience. In all this he belongs to us and those whom he was certainly willing to have as sharers in his mother's milk* he does not shut out from the rewards of his obedience. I beseech you not to desert him and flee away when he begins to be fearful and weary and sad as death approaches, and when he himself has been willing to be given into the hands of wicked men,* but let us, when he is dragged to insult, go with him, our hearts closely knit to his. For being sold he redeems us, being betrayed he guards us, being stripped he clothes us and because he does not refuse, though undeservedly, to be scourged, spit upon and mocked, he keeps from us the everlasting shame we have deserved. Because his face is covered

*E.g. Mt 8-9,
Mk 4-5,
Cf. Lk 7:22,
Mt 11:5

*E.g. Mt 14:15-21,

*Cf. Sg 8:1

*Cf. Ep 14, p. 188
below. Cf. Collect
for Triduum

and smitten, because he is saluted with ridicule with bended knee, because for him a crown of thorns is woven, from us is banished everlasting dishonor. Because the cross is laid on him to bear, because he is cast forth from the city, because his whole body is stretched on the wood of the cross, because his body is pierced with lance and nails, for this the sentence of eternal malediction is revoked.*

*Jn 19. Cf. Mt 27: 26-50, Mk 15: 15-37, Lk 23: 26-46

36. See now that from the body of the Lamb flow five most needful streams. We have two on the feet, two on the hands, and the fifth flows from the opening on his side. Come, dear friend, let us drink with joy from the Saviour's fount.*

*Cf. Is 12:3

37. But perhaps you say: From my Lord's wounds I see flowing blood not water.* I reply: From the side of Christ blood and water are believed to have flowed. Although the blood of Christ—which heals by its own worth—redeems and crowns, there is water in it, because it cleanses, restores and cools. It cleanses us from sin, it restores us through hope, it cools us from the heat of fleshy lust. But waters are drunk from the Saviour's founts when the streams of grace are drawn by the lips of faith from the wounds of Christ. So the wounds in his feet are fountains, but fountains of oil: the wounds in his hands are balm, the wound in his side is a fountain of wine. 'How,' you ask 'since from such places nothing but blood is seen to flow?' Hear how this is. Oil heals, balm gives forth fragrance, wine inebriates. Oil is

*Cf. Jn 19:34

mercy, which the guilty one receives at the feet of Jesus when with humility he seeks for pardon. You see the oil drip from his feet. Balm, because it flows from the fountains of his hands, is the precious esteem for virtue which the righteous man takes from the generosity of Christ. It is enough for the guilty one if he gains pardon: it is not enough for the righteous if he does not earn glory for his virtues. Mercy offers the one [pardon] to him who is humbly prostrated at his feet. Generosity bestows the other [glory] on him who is raised by the virtue of his soul to receive the great gift from his hands. But from the wine cellar of his pierced side there pours forth abundantly the wine of life-giving charity. And surely if Christ is the true vine, if his flesh is the grape of the vine, how will the blood which flows down from his flesh not be the wine? Or how would his bride the church please her bridegroom in his marriage, if she did not possess in the sacred mysteries this wine coming from Christ himself? This is the wine which makes glad the heart of man,* while the blood of Christ produces in the soul the intoxication of a sober love. But what, dear friend, do we do? Why do we not rush to embrace him as he hangs there since he himself invites us with arms outstretched? Why do we not draw near to kiss him, we who see his calm face exposed and disposed towards us? Why do we not at once suck the breasts of his wounds, most of all those in the feet before which

*Cf. Ps 104:15

we lie prostrate? See, he who consoles us has returned to the Father and, as one truly obedient, with head inclined, has received permission to return. He receives, as it were, permission to return when with head inclined he yielded up his spirit.

38. The good shepherd departs,* the wise teacher, the sweet Lord, the gentle friend, the tender father—and we orphans, what shall we do? You see that physical nature endures not his departure from the body but turns wholly to lamentation. The sun was darkened* because at the setting of the true light it showed the mien of a mourner. There is earthquake, the rocks are riven, the veil of the temple is destroyed,* a kind of revolt of the elements is manifested at the death of their creator. Alas! How comfortless would be our desolation did we not trust that resurrection was at hand. Soon he will rise from the dead. It is good not to leave the tomb, but with the blessed women let us buy spices to anoint his dead body.* May Jesus, returning from hell, find us with fragrant spices, so that with the spices of pity and mercy, we may embalm his body—that is, the members of the church, especially the downcast and the poor. O when risen love has given himself again to the beloved Magdalen, may he not refuse to let us become sharers in her joy. Happy are we if the brightness of his resurrection shines upon our hearts: if, the leaven of malice and wickedness being purged away, we may eat with holy eagerness the unleavened

*Cf. Vigils of Holy Saturday, Responsory of Nocturn 1V

*Lk 23:45

*Cf. Mt 27:51

*Cf. Mk 16:1, Lk 23:56

bread of sincerity,* the flesh of Christ.

*I Co 5:8

39. We must, however, beware lest the wild lettuce be missing from our feast,* for that joy which neither the bitterness of death nor the fear of sin disturbs ought to be afraid of the danger from arrogance. If therefore in this our soleminity we rejoice with trembling* and if no ingratitude arising from the leaven of pride finds a place in our ways, after the fulfilment of our joy in the resurrection it will be granted us to experience the coming of the Holy Spirit. The Holy Spirit is love, and it is fitting, dear friend, that my discourse should end where it began. I began, it's true, with love. I wished to write out of a great love and I have said what I could about love. Sweet is the subject of love, sweet and very sweet is affection, and where duty is so sweet, sweet too will be its reward. Holy love looks for no other reward and desires no other glory than that it should have the strength to merit its fulness. It will be fulfilled when Jesus, the source of love, has burst forth from the paradise of pleasure so that a flood of glory works in those who love him. Let us love him and let us love one another in him, for there is nothing in life happier than to love faithfully and be loved in return.

*Cf. Ex 12:8

*Cf. Ps 2:11

Let love of the world in no way draw us from this love, for love of the world is not love but madness. Love of the world disturbs or carries away right feeling, drains off the heart's health and in resisting the wisdom of Christ it simply acts as a madman. Our head is Christ.* The thought of his head is love of heavenly things, and to wish for or to engage in any others is the mark of madness not of love. I shall leave you therefore in the love of heavenly things and I can leave you nowhere better though I shall not cease to love you with this love as mine. I shall love you, I say, as far as the love of the world allows me, because I admit I am not without experience of that oft-mentioned folly. Unhappy as I am, I am attached to the cares of the world under the pretext of religion and I who had sworn to despise the world often fall back into Egypt. Though in my body remaining in the church, in my thoughts I wander round what is worldly, and when I ought—and seem—to be pondering on things eternal, my whole being is being carried into the circle of the temporal. Help your friend, help him, I pray. And see that the supplications of your sons be joined to the urgency of your prayer. This is the proof of true love, if we offer our souls to Christ on behalf of those whom we love in Christ. But especially remember me when the Lamb without spot* is sacrificed, for this is more acceptable than whole burnt offerings.

40. In my name greet the venerable prior whom affection for me has touched and the love of Christ has wounded. Greet your mother, very dear to me, more truly your brother by faith and love than by the flesh. Greet that monk whose name escapes me, but, God willing, not his soul, which

Cf. 1 Co 11:3, Ep 5:23

Ex 12:5, Lv 9:3, 1 P 1:19

he thought he had placed in my heart, Greet that young man who has so deeply sucked in honey from the rock* which is Christ as to derive from Peter both his name and his steadfast soul.* Greet him in whom is grace, who is in harmony with the grace of God both by his name and by his devotion.* Greet G. the doorkeeper, who standing at the gates of justice will bring me some heavenly gift. Greet the guest master, who not only ministers with devotion to earthly guests, but has made within himself a lodging-place for Christ. Greet the whole company of your holy community, who, binding me to them in holy charity, are gathered together into my heart.

*Cf. Dt 32:13

*Cf. Mt 16:18

*A monk named Gratian?

41. Above and before all else, greet for me that soul which you know is most closely bound and known to me, who derives her name indeed from the name of the lamb and is fired by the flames of the Holy Spirit.† To her you will commend me wholly, you will give to her my whole self; and though in holy love I am wholly hers, yet you will renew this affection by calling it to mind anew. Impress upon her the perfect love of God and contempt of the world, the shunning of the praise of men, avoidance of familiarity with seculars, so that she may cling more closely to her spouse in proportion as the world claims nothing of her. Let her stand and entreat before God on behalf of my failings, for her

†Agnes, the future abbess of the Cistercian nuns 'les clairets' founded in the diocese of Chartes in 1213. Adam addressed to her some letters not yet edited or translated.

lovely charity holds my whole self in the Lord. Let her greet in my name all those souls who she knows love us, for we need the love of all the virtuous. That sweet soul cannot be more profitably reminded of me than if this poor letter be shown to her. Farewell and may her sanctity continue to be made perfect in the Lord. Farewell in the Lord to you all.

LETTER IV
TO
MARGARET,

Virgin of Christ,*
from Brother Adam, sinner—
pleasure to the Spouse of virgins through
the unfading lily of chastity.

**A nun of Fontevrault in Normandy and sister
of Henry I, count of Champagne.*

LETTER IV
42

AS WE ARE BOUND to love Christ, so we ought to reverence and honor his temples. Now his dwelling place is chastity undefiled, most of all that which true love of Christ has sanctified. Truly it is in gardens and among lilies that Christ the Lord, the flower of the field and lily of the valley,* is found to flourish. May the rose be not absent from the lily, so that the whiteness of chastity may be tinged with the red hue of charity. How lovely are the cheeks of one in whom producing beauty complete, love joins virtue, charity joins chastity. The grace of such beauty attracts him who is lovely beyond the sons of men,* and truly happy is that soul whose beauty wins favor in his eyes. The elegance of Queen Esther was most pleasing to Ahasuerus* because the innocence of her character set off the loveliness of her countenance. Innocent character, unsullied thoughts, just deeds, praiseworthy regard for discipline make the soul worthy of the kisses and embrace of the Creator. A touch to be revered, a marriage to be honored,

*Cf. Sg 2:1 :
Bernard, SC 47;
OB 2:62-66,
William Cant, I, 9,
107-113
(CF 6:86-91)

*Ps 45:2

*Cf. Est 2

Letter IV

from which is excluded every stain, in which no corruption finds a place. Happy the offspring which has come forth from such a union, which being conceived by the Holy Spirit is nourished by the breasts of holy mother church. Those breasts are filled with heaven, dropping the milk of spiritual teaching,* from which purity of feeling, innocency of character proceed to the full-grown strength and complete understanding of the love of God.

*Cf. 1 P 2:2

43. I think that by God's grace you have reached this age in that you no longer play by Christ's cradle as one sharing Christ's milk, but, being ready to be crucified with Christ,* you are able to eat more solid food.† Because of the words of his lips you desire and are able to keep to the hard paths,* boasting, after the example of Christ crucified, in the glory of his cross.† If you have not shrunk from being united with your spouse in such a bed, you will one day reach the joy of the marriage-chamber, which knows nothing of cross and hardship. I beseech you, dear friend, that when, in your Jesus, it has gone well with you,* you intercede with him for my sins. When that joyous splendor has smiled upon you more generously than usual, commend your friend to your beloved, that through your activity and prayer he may be able with you to take hold of him whom I adore and love in you. Farewell.

*Cf. Gal 2:19
†Cf. I Co 3:2, Hb 5:12-14
*Ps 17:4
†Cf. Ga 6:14

*Gn 40:14

LETTER V
TO
OSMUND,

Monk of Mortemer,*
his dear brother in Christ, Brother Adam,
Abbot of Perseigne—
virtuous life and strength in the Lord.

*Mortemer, a Cistercian abbey in Normandy.

LETTER V

44

SHREWDLY DOES the reflection of a prudent mind consider that it should not dare to ask for what may offend the spirit of the request, or go beyond its strength. Truly importunity is the mother of boredom. The more tiresomely it continues to press its requests the more it believes that what it is seeking is opportune. How does it happen, I beg you, how does it happen that you think me greater than I am and thus you have become importunate to one who loves you. You are indeed loved, but not perhaps to the degree you think. Because, though you may be worthy of love, I cannot expend upon a human being a measure of love which I am unable to give to the Creator himself.

45. Still, somehow I love what is worth loving as far as I recognize it. But the result of my effort does not always prove adequate witness to my loving feeling. The man in whom feeling corresponds closely with action can easily perform what is requested of him. But I do not deserve to be renewed by God to such a degree that

these two good things can be found in me. My affection is limited, my knowledge trifling, my pursuits manifold, my griefs many, my mental and physical toil beyond my strength. What has the preoccupation of Martha to do with the leisure of Mary? Or how do you seek in Leah, who is full of toil and blear-eyed, the elegance of Rachel?* † Your estimate of me, my son, is cheating you, and your love makes too much of me. Meanwhile the substitution of Leah can not bring you what you long to get from the eyes of Rachel. Old words have not yet departed from my lips,* old habits have not yet been rubbed away from my mind. And you are urging me to discourse on the newness of life, how those recently turned away from the world can be changed into new men.

*Lk 10:38-42, Gn 39

*1 S 2:3

46. In fact, it is essential that those who turn from the world should with great care be shaped by the splendor of the new life, so that, putting off the old man,* they should rightly be called 'novices' as the name implies.* But how can this be taught by me, for I was never a novice in our order. I have not proven fit to learn it by experience or apply the teaching to others. Of course I do not deny that I have at some time been a master of novices. But I could not adequately instruct beginners in the rules of this art, for it was without experience that I assumed the office.

*Cf. Ep 4:22, Col 3:9

*new men

---

†Martha and Leah are traditional types of the active life, while Mary and Rachel symbolize the contemplative life. Cf Gregory the Great, *Homilia in Ezech.* 2.2.10; PL 76:953-4.

47. Be that as it may, for this task I think there are six essentials. If these are held and observed, the Ethiopian can change his skin* and become white with a blessed newness. The first is fervent faith, the second the fear of God, the third love of wisdom, the fourth the devout bearing of his novice master: the fifth the dutiful anxiety of the master regarding the noviciate, the sixth friendly conversation on spiritual matters and regular observances.

*Jr 13:23

48. Faith drives out ignorance and promotes understanding. Isaiah says: 'Unless you believe you will not understand.'* For he who does not believe does not see the light of the knowledge of God and therefore is not moved by fear or love of the one whom he does not deserve to understand.

*Is 7:9 (LXX)

49. The effect of the fear of God is twofold. It puts an end to malice and is the beginning of wisdom. Of the first effect it was written: 'The fear of God drives out sin,'* and again: 'The fear of the Lord works no evil.'* Of the second effect the Psalmist says: 'Holy and terrible is his name. The fear of the Lord is the beginning of wisdom.'* Where wisdom begins, malice rightly comes to an end because wisdom overcomes malice. How happy is the beginning of wisdom that drives out all carelessness and folly. As it is written: 'He who fears the Lord is in nothing negligent'* and therefore not slothfully does he resist malice.

*Si 1:27
*Pr 8:13,
Cf. Rm 13:10

*Ps 111:9-10

*Qo 7:19

50. The love of wisdom, which comes third, through affection produces care for

the things which should be known or done, and eagerly completes and perfects justice. The innocency of the soul which fear restores, love preserves. When to this it adds deeds of justice it carries one on to the contemplation of things eternal. For the rest, the lover of this wisdom can justly, and should, be called 'philosopher', for while the light of truth illumines him, love of virtue also delights him.

51. In the fourth place is put the novice master's religious demeanor. This should be presented to the novice as in a mirror. When there is set before him close at hand an example of good conduct, he is stimulated move effectively to desire to imitate it. On the mount Moses was shown a model, in whose likeness he had to frame the tabernacle.* So lofty must be the life of superiors that the demeanor of the subordinates may be fashioned after their example.

*Ex 26:1-30

52. In the fifth place is set the careful anxiety of the master for the novitiate, by which he proves and tests whether he [the novice] should be considered able and willing for the *opus dei*, for the enduring of reproach, for the virtue of obedience.* Surely if the master has found him ready for these three things, if he has known him to be fervent in the *opus dei*; if he possesses a good and joyful soul, showing the good standard of obedience to his superiors, his equals, and his inferiors:* if he is patient in bearing insults, he can know that he is truly seeking

*Cf. RB 58:7

*RB 71:1

God*—provided this happy beginning does not fail to end in an equally happy perseverance.

53. Let the master teach him to persevere fervently in the divine office, that he may guard against the sentence of malediction which the Holy Spirit calls down upon all who insincerely and slothfully perform the *opus dei*.* Is he not insincere whose soul is out of harmony with his tongue, and when he appears to honor God with his lips is not afraid to withdraw from him through voluptuous or even malicious thoughts? The Holy Spirit, through the prophet, rebukes evil praises of this kind, saying: 'This people honors me with its lips, but their hearts are far from me. Therefore in vain do they worship me.'* The lips of one who praises God should be well-sounding cymbals. But the cymbals do not sound well when the intention and affection of the heart do not accord with the lips that are uttering the praises. He is a slothful praiser who is careless in God's praise. Small wonder if the lethargy of sloth is in one who, being dead at heart, performs God's praises with the mere sound of his tongue. He who so behaves when praising God brings upon himself the curse pronounced by the Holy Spirit. Therefore the novices should be earnestly warned lest those who have come to understand the blessing of God fall into the snare of this curse.

54. The master's affectionate care must teach the novices the importance of the

*RB 58:7

*Cf. Jr 48:10

*Cf. Mt 15:8,
Is 29:13,
Cf. Ps 78:36

of the obedience which should be given to their superiors as if to God, in accordance with the rule,* to their equals out of brotherly love, to inferiors out of the virtue of humility. He who loves his brother out of charity and denies himself out of humility minds but little if he suffers from insults heaped upon him, but rather, crucifying himself for Christ, he is glad that he shares in the shame of the cross. Therefore it is in his fervor in the *opus dęi* that he shows that he loves the worship of God, in making plain his obedience he shows that he loves his neighbour, in his patient bearing of insults he shows that he has denied himself.

*Cf. RB 2:1, 5:15

55. In the sixth place is set friendly and frequent conversation on spiritual matters or on the observance of the Rule. Those who are newly converted from the world, however strong they are in devotion, often suffer from the sin of *accidie*, and because of this the friendly and frequent talks of the master on spiritual matters must counter the discontent which is wont to arise from *accidie*.

56. Meanwhile there must be conference on spiritual subjects or on the mysteries of the Scriptures or on the examples of the saints or on the rewards of heaven—how they are gained by good works—or on the torments of hell, which the dread severity of divine justice threatens to inflict upon those who are slaves to uncleanness and injustice. To talk of these matters frequently, to meditate on them

together, deeply moves and inspires the soul, so that is raised above its vices and sins and eagerly presses on to works of virtue.

57. Again, from friendly, frequent and good conversation is born a kind of worthy intimacy by which the master is rendered bolder to reprove and the one reproved more ready to submit to instruction. Each becomes more skilled in understanding the Scriptures, the novice more practised in his observance of the Rule. It follows that now the master ought, according to the rule, not indeed to lay upon him, but to tell him, of the harsh and bitter way that leads to God.* This is nothing other than to show from the Scriptures and from suitable examples the strait, steep road which leads to life.* This road doubtless he does not tread who does not strive to enter by the narrow gate according to the precept of the Lord. 'Strive', says the Lord, 'to enter through the narrow gate.'* And in another place: 'Steep and narrow is the way that leads to life'.* And holy David: 'Because of the words of thy lips I have kept the hard ways'.* What, I ask, can be harder in the way of the Lord than to deny oneself, take up the cross,* submit one's whole will to that of another? What, I say, can be harder on the road that leads to God than to inflict pain upon the flesh with its defects and desires and to show the world crucified to oneself and oneself to the world?* This surely all do who wish truly to belong to Christ. 'Those who are Christ's,' says the

*RB 58:8

*Cf. Mt 7:14

*Lk 13:24

*Mt 7:14

*Ps 17:4

*Mt 16:24, Mk 8:34, Lk 9:23

*Cf. Ga 6:14

apostle, 'have crucified the flesh with its sins and desires.'* *Ga 5:24

58. Therefore the master teaches the novice the harsh and rugged way by which one comes to God,* when he points out to him both by his example and his preaching that the way of salvation is narrow and steep.* If this way of salvation is so narrow, so steep, it is Christ the Lord: narrow because of the humility of the flesh he took, steep because of the foulness of sin. For he did no sin, neither was guile found in his mouth.* He who in imitation of his humility has not shown himself as a little child does not advance upon this way.* He will not be able to climb that steep path who has willed to burden himself with the load of sin or love of the visible world. Hence it comes that to men weighed down with the burdens of this Babylon, the Holy Spirit cries by the prophet: 'Sons of men, how long will you be heavy-hearted? Why do you love vanity and seek falsehood? Know that the Lord has exalted his saint.'* Rightly has the saint been exalted for he is not crushed beneath the burdens of worldly misery; so that while he takes no pleasure in what is vain and transitory, he leaps over it with his whole heart and receives the spirit of freedom. For where the spirit of the Lord is, there is freedom.* Freedom, I tell you, from sin, from necessity, from misery.* That spirit is sent forth from God; our character is remade, the face of the earth renewed.† And you will be able to rejoice over your novices when virtue from

*RB 58:8

*Mt 7:14

*1 P 2:22

*Cf. Mt 18:3, Mk 10:15

*Ps 4:2-3

*2 Co 3:17

*Cf. Bernard, Gra II, 7; OB 3:171
†Cf. Ps 104:30

above makes them sharers in this wondrous renewal. They will rightly be called novices when by this renewal the wedding garment is fitted upon them. For the rest, they will not be cast out from the marriage of the Lamb when they shine forth in the marriage garment to the honor of the Bridegroom and Bride.*

*Cf. Rv 19:7-9

59. This wedding garment is the splendor and glory of an inward renewal. This garment is made up of three things: chastity of body, heart-felt love, a comeliness derived from discipline. In this garment, the cloth made from wool betokens, so to speak, chastity because it knows not physical passion. Love is likened to the skins which are added to the cloth that the garment may become warmer. These skins the capacity for suffering and the deathlessness of the spotless lamb have brought to us. For the love which he had for us he gave skin for skin,* and all that he might have possessed [he gave] for his life, that is for the deliverance of his church which he loved as his own life, even more than his life. The border set on the garment as an ornament is the splendor and beauty of discipline. When this is outwardly observed in irreproachable fashion, through it there seems to be symbolized a disposition towards charity and love. This is the garment the bride had put on and to her the bridegroom in the book of wisdom cried out: 'How beautiful is a chaste begetting accompanied by light.'* So in a psalm she asks to be taught about disci-

*Jb 2:4

*Ws 4:1

pline, desiring to be built up with the goodness of continence and of charity. 'Teach me,' she says, 'goodness and discipline and knowledge because I have believed in your commandments.'* Having gained, sometime, the discipline which she prayed for she said: 'I have come early to maturity and I have cried out.'* For discipline makes a man mature; it is the ordered movement of all his members and seemly comportment in every attitude and action.

*Ps 119:66

*Cf. Ps 119:147

60. Therefore briefly to repeat what has been said: it is essential for the novice to begin with faith. This truly withdraws his mind from the darkness of ignorance and incorporates him into Christ. Being incorporated into Christ he is made believing and faithful, belief leading to confidence in the promises, and faith to the keeping of the commandments. Fear reveals a fitting penitence for past sins and also shuts out the evils that attempt to enter the heart. Love of wisdom carefully guards the innocence regained through fear and does not cease to add justice to this very innocence by its zeal for a most dutiful generosity. The godly conversation of the master, by the example it gives of integrity, rouses the novice to be eager to emulate his virtue. His tender care for his pupil carefully considers, as much as it can, the inward and outward condition of the man so that according to what he sees in him he may know how to show his approval or to come down to his level. It is

written: 'Carefully examine the appearance of your flock.'* Friendly spiritual conversation, as had been said, advisedly fights against the evil of *accidie*, because the more a soul becomes accustomed to holy conversation the more the flaming words melt it. The bride accustomed to the divine communication says: 'My soul is melted when my beloved has spoken.'*

*Pr 27:23

*Sg 5:6

61. Surely in these six points is contained almost the whole education of the devout soul, so in these six which have been mentioned let him exercise himself in his time of probation, and his probation completed, let him limit himself to those three which are set out in the formula of his profession. For stability and conversion of character and obedience according to the rule are solemnly promised in the formula of his votive profession* and in these three that proceed from the oft-mentioned six is contained a kind of perfection. For by means of the curb of stability promised, we are tethered like pious mules to the heavenly crib. By conversion of character we come to imitate the purity of angels. By showing obedience we copy the very ministry of angels. And so faith and fear have a care for the establishment of stability. Loving the virtues and following the example of the master lead to conversion of character. The attentive care of the master and the friendly interchange of spiritual conversation lead to shaping the desired obedience. For when through spiritual intercourse the

*Cf. RB 58:17

sloth of *accidie* is put to flight, the soul revives to the fervor of obedience.

62. To the last question which you yourself propounded, you have, I think adequately replied. Often with God and with those who under God have the care of others it happens in the ordering of affairs that a gentle person's patience is tortured when he is faced with an irritating person. Sometimes when that has come about through good intent, a two-fold fruit results: for the one who suffers the trial there comes from the reproof an increase of merit, and he who before seemed incorrigible is restored to health through the good example.

63. Thus the apostle is allowed by God to be beaten, not that by that means an assault of this kind might preserve his humility but that the whole church of Christ might bear with patience the blows that come from God, following that example, and so gain humility. Did Christ, the head of the church, not endure under the eye of the sun blows, insults, the cross and death—all unmerited—and through the example of his passion and the price of his blood recall the lost from everlasting death? Mark, too, the patience of innocent Job: to what afflictions he is subjected by the ordinance of God, not only that the patience of a righteous man may be proved invincible but that an unhappy world may by his righteous example be trained to patience in its adversities. But if at times trials fall upon one to the glory of God, as

Christ our Lord says in the gospel happened to the man born blind,* is it not for a useful purpose that an innocent man suffers affliction from God or from man, since the glory of God is made manifest by the light of his patience? 'Let your light shine before men,' says the Lord, 'that they may see your good works and glorify your father who is in heaven.'* Therefore it often happens that the master, of set purpose, blames rather harshly someone of whose patience he is confident in the presence of someone perverse. Because when evil men gaze upon God, who is wonderful in his saints, they are changed from their former perversity into another man through the patience which these [saints] show, and the innocence they bear, and through the gentleness of their devotion.

*Jn 9:1-3

*Mt 5:16

64. See, brother, prevailed upon by pressure from you, I have said something, but perhaps I have hardly satisfied your expectation. For more copious streams cannot flow from a narrow pipe. Nevertheless, if, as you declare, you love me truly in Christ, intercede, I beseech you, with God for my sins and commend me earnestly to those who, so far as you know, are controlled and influenced by Christian piety. Greet your novices in my name and on my behalf advise them so to direct their minds to a holy novitiate that with heart and soul they may renounce the worldly past.

LETTER VI
TO
OSMUND,

*Monk of Mortemer,
his dear brother in Christ:
brother Adam, servant of the servants of
God, who serves Christ at Perseigne,
sends greeting and perseverance
in true religion.*

LETTER VI
65

WHEN ANY HONORABLE REQUEST is made by a friend, and it is a friend who is asked, such a request ought not to suffer refusal, provided that the ability to fulfil it is not lacking. Trusting to the seemliness of the request and our close friendship, you beg with great earnestness to be roused to enthusiasm for virtue by means of letters. If you are well-disposed and of your own will inclined to what is right, a friend's encouragement will not injure your desire for progress. If perchance your disposition is slower than it should be in pursuit of the good, still perhaps exhortation will supply a remedy for the disease. In any case, the word of salvation is profitable to the listener, especially when he who speaks loves, and when there is no doubt that the one to whom he speaks loves in return.

66. And what except love should be the theme in the conversations of friends? That love, I mean, which comes into no suspicion if it is called affection or charity. The word 'love' is common to widely

differing things. But the word 'charity' is restricted to those things alone that possess the essence of truth and virtue. Since therefore God is rightly and specifically called 'love' or 'charity' or 'affection', what more suitable theme, what sweeter talk would there be between us than love of this kind?

67. Since the fear of God is the beginning of wisdom* and to love God is itself wisdom, it is clear that the savor of holy love arises from the desire for the fear of God. The fear of God clears the soul's dwelling place of vices, and when their bitterness has been driven out it restores to the heart a longing for wisdom. Thenceforward the soul begins to hunger and thirst for righteousness. Surely it would in no wise so hunger did not the savor already experienced call forth the hunger. 'Those who eat me,' says Wisdom, 'will still hunger and those who drink me will still thirst.'* For what is the love of righteousness but a kind of delight in wisdom, since to be righteous is nothing other than to be seasoned with divine savors and anointed with divine perfumes. Are the character and works of the righteous not the perfumes of the virtues, which they are seen to derive from their inward delight in the dish of wisdom? Wisdom derives its name from 'savor'* because it makes one taste the things that are above and because it is the delicious seasoning of character. What therefore is sweeter in life than to fear God and through the careful service of the

*Cf. Ps 111:10, Pr 9:10, Si 1:13

*Si 24:29

*sapienta—sapor

fear of God to prepare in the soul a dwelling-place for the love of God? Truly fear's solicitude keeps the mind in complete safety so that the joyful festival of love celebrates there its solemn holidays.* The soul needs to be at leisure so that it can be free and able to see how great is the sweetness of God and to experience what is the festival of holy love.

*Cf. Aelred. Spec car 3.1; Pl 195: 575 D

68. There are seven solemn festivals when one is at leisure for God and in which the soul keeps holiday from all servile work that it may be more free for God. The first festival is the spirit of the fear of the Lord which puts an end to sin and vice. For the fear of the Lord is in nothing negligent* and, while it curses the mud and Pharaoh's bricks and Egypt's straw,* it is already preparing to have leisure for the Lord.†

*Cf. Qo 7:19

*Cf. Ex 5

69. The second festival is the spirit of piety in which God is worshipped more truly and heartily the longer the excitement of a wearying perversity is shut out from the soul. Piety indeed is the worship of God and sympathy for one's neighbor, and in this festival there begins that calm, that silence which is called by the prophet 'the cult of righteousness'.* Observe that in this silence which is called the cult of righteousness, which is kept in heaven,* that is in the soul of the righteous, Michael does battle with the dragon. The quieter the heart has been from the tension of

*Is 32:17

*Rv 8:1. Cf. Gregory the Great, Hom. in Ezech. 2.3.14; Pl 76: 957A, CCSL 2.3.14: 152:235.

†On the vocabulary of holy leisure, see Jean Leclercq, *Otia Monastica.* Studia Anselmiana, 51. (Rome, 1953) Translation projected for Cistercian Fathers Series, No. 53.

servile toil, so much the more does spiritual wickedness disturb it. One rightly asks how there has been silence in heaven* when a battle, and such a battle, is fought there. A battle, he says, was fought in heaven. Michael and his angels fought with the dragon.* Notice that heaven is the soul of the righteous: in this heaven silence is kept when the soul is at peace from the noise of the world* and, being free from any impulse towards sin, takes its whole delight in worship and the love of righteousness. Yet that peace in which the soul is renewing itself to the likeness of God does not mean that it need do no battle with ethereal powers. 'Michael' means 'who is like God.' By this name is meant the likeness to God which righteousness alone preserves. Truly Paul was living in this silence of the spirit, was celebrating there festivals of love when he spoke thus of himself and of those like him: 'Our wrestling is not against flesh and blood but against the rulers of this darkness, against spiritual wickedness in heavenly places.'*

*Rv 8:1

*Cf. Rv 12:7

*Cf. William. Contemp. 4; Pl 184:372D, Cf. 3:48

*Eph 6:12

70. The third festival is the spirit of knowledge which, it is clear, enlightens the righteous soul with knowledge of the truth and instructs it on how to teach its neighbor. He who has been worthy inwardly to learn these good things ought to utter them and teach them abroad. He to whom it has been given to know God and himself ought not in his teaching to disregard the progress of his neighbors. Surely this spirit of knowledge is not unapprovingly called a festival,

for he who has obtained it keeps holiday from all errors and false doctrines. This knowledge must not be understood as being that which according to the Apostle 'puffs up' for it always edifies* because of its harmony with the devotion which goes with it.

*1 Co 8:1

71. The fourth festival is the spirit of fortitude in which begins love strong as death.* When it has fallen into diverse temptations it is wont to consider even this all joy. They keep this festival to whom James the Apostle said: 'Think it all joy, beloved brethren, when you have fallen into diverse temptations.* He who lives in the spirit of fortitude either does not feel the untoward thing that has happened or else easily overcomes it by unwearied virtue.

*Cf. Sg 8:6

*Jm 1:2

72. The fifth festival is the spirit of counsel. It is a small thing for it to fulfil God's commands but with great eagerness of heart it is busily engaged in aspiring to follow God's counsels. For after you have fulfilled God's commands, if according to the Apostle's exhortation you strive after the better gifts,* you stretch yourself to fulfil the counsels which are set by the Saviour before those who are eager for perfection. Therefore to him who said that from his youth he had kept the commandments of God, the Lord says in that gospel: 'You lack one thing. If you want to be perfect, go, sell everything you have and give to the poor and come follow me.'* He therefore lives in this festival, that is in the

*Cf. 1 Co 12:31, Mk 10:20-21, Lk 18:21-22

*Mt 19:20-21

spirit of counsel, who does nothing without counsel and is eager to give good counsel to everyone in need. For he has in him the spirit of counsel, and the angel of mighty counsel, the angel of Christ, teaches him.

73. The sixth festival is the spirit of understanding in which the soul, by keeping the former festivals, has been fully taught to fix its thoughts on what is invisible. Cleansed and purified, as has been said, by the keeping of the preceding festivals it is fitted by meditation to dwell with the heavenly realities and, with pictures of the world removed from the mind, to bring the understanding to invisible realities. For understanding is the simple and clear knowledge of all that is invisible.

74. The seventh festival, that is the sabbath, is the spirit of wisdom, where the soul, now enlightened by divine splendor, begins to taste from time to time a kind of relish of flavor. Here now the soul is divinely taught to know the things that are above, to seek out the things that are above, while learning by experience how great, how wonderful is the sweetness of the inward flavor.

75. Note that the festival which is called understanding is in brilliant light so completely that he who attains to it becomes nothing less than the cherubim, that is the fullness of knowledge. But that festival which is called the spirit of wisdom consists entirely of flavor, so that the one who deservedly attains it is nothing less than the seraphim, that is burning and

blazing.* He whom love for God has kindled, being melted by this heat, doubtless kindles others. To this ardor had come that soul keeping festival which said: 'my soul melted when my beloved spoke.'* The spirit which the fire of this love melts sets others aflame, while from its own melting making known how greatly it loves them.

Cf. Gregory the Great, Homil. in Evang. 2.35.10; PL 27:1252AB

*Sg 5:6 (Vulg.)

76. Now there are very many meltings of the soul which is on fire with heavenly desire, and which inflames others to long for this desire. Firstly it melts into tears of compunction through the office and the pressure of the initial fear. For with this fear which is the beginning of wisdom* is mingled the love of righteousness. Secondly, it melts into tears of devotion which are want to rise from the recollection of spiritual benefit. For when it recalls God's favors which, though unworthy, it has received, it is moved to tears and gives thanks. Thirdly, it melts into tears of love which arise from the hope and burning desire to see one day the face of the Creator. Fourthly, it melts into tears of pity which are produced by the feeling of compassion for the misery of its brethren. The fifth melting comes when the soul pours out its whole self in fervent love and expends itself on the good works of the active life. The sixth comes when the whole soul melts and dissolves into the delights of heavenly contemplation. Concerning such a soul it is written: 'Who is she that rises from the desert overflowing with delight?'* The seventh is when such a soul

*Cf. Ps 111:10, Pr 9:10, Cf. Si 1:13

*Sg 8:5

flows down and melts with the fragrance of its good name and for the consolation of many strews it about to make a sweet savor of fragrant renown so that of it may be said: 'Your name is perfume poured forth.'* Such a soul is called in the Song of Songs a column of smoke perfumed with myrrh and frankincense and the unguents of every powder,* such a soul by its fragrance draws others and makes them run after it towards the love of God, full of joy and saying: 'We will run after you in the fragrance of your perfumes.'* Meltings of this kind are those breaths for which the bride is praised when by the voice of the bridegroom in the Canticle is said: 'Your breaths are a garden of ripe apples with their fruits.'*

*Cf. Sg 1:2

*Sg 3:6

*Sg 1:3

*Sg 4:13

77. But to those good things, my friend, never do they come who do not derive their innocence from the fear of God. Nor can they rejoice in the birth of righteousness in whom the fear of God does not create the seed of innocence. But fear does not by such conception make fruitful those who are not enlightened by the splendor of a true faith. Believe me, that you may hear the words of God with affectionate feeling; hear, that you may perform his commands. For from the fulfilling of the commands follows the happy attainment of the rewards. Fear God, therefore, and keep his commandments. This is the whole duty of man.* Farewell always in God and so live that your conscience may inwardly bear testimony to you and you may outwardly be strong to

*Qo 12:13

be an example to your brethren.

LETTER VII
TO
OSMUND,

Monk of Mortemer,
his dear brother in Christ:
brother Adam servant of the servants of
God who fights at Perseigne,
gives greeting in the Holy Spirit.

LETTER VII
78

IMPORTUNITY IS THE MOTHER of boredom when it is not excused by the warmer sincerity of friendship. Nothing is bolder than true friendship, and it does not think anything more fitting than to press unreasonably upon him in whom it trusts. Such confidence gives the friends of God their perseverance in prayer. And they do not fail in constancy in their prayer because they know that they trust in him whom they love. You seem to have this loving trust in me. And therefore you are not afraid that you will be reproved for boring me, because consciousness of the love within you gives you confidence.

79. But why, pray, do you complain so bitterly to me about yourself, and set before me the different weaknesses of your soul, as if thus placing them in the way of cure? What profit can there be in revealing a disease to someone suffering the same infirmity? Does the one who reveals his laments and tears to another; whom he ought rather to console, not increase somehow the sick man's pain? You ought rather

to disclose your weakness to one who has been given virtue and health of soul, and to whom along with health of soul has been given skill in healing. One who achieves health of soul, namely virtue, does not for that reason possess immediately the skill to heal. He who receives both from God is at hand for those who are sick and successfully heals them. For it is absurd that anyone should practice the art of medicine and show himself half-hearted towards those on whom he expends his care. The man whom the marks of palpable indifference render contemptible can hardly be successful in offering remedies.

80. Since therefore the health of the soul is virtue and its sickness vice, I do not offer you a remedy for your sickness because I am lying constantly in the infirmary, suffering from this same disease of the world's misery. Truly, because the heart is guarded negligently, life abounds and super-abounds in sin and from indifference is born a poisonous offspring of faults because of acquiescence in the streams of vices. The inward clinging to sin indeed means that there is in us almost continually a remembrance of wrong-doing. Yet if this has with it no pleasure or consent, nothing results from it but warfare for those who love God. If the soul continues firm in the virtue of perseverance, from the warfare comes forth victory and victory goes forward to the crown which only the person who does not strive lawfully fails to deserve.* Therefore the

*Cf. 2 Tm 2:5

virtuous soul, because it cannot oppose the first strivings, takes care at least not to fall into the danger of feeling pleasure or consenting, and not at any time because of its proximity to be drawn into sinful action.

81. But my unhappy soul is from habit constantly shaken by these first strivings and it is lured into danger by the thoughts that arise from them, and my pleasure and consent grow strong from this sickness so that often they draw me to an act of forbidden consent. Oh if only, as wisdom counsels, the heart were to be kept safe by complete vigilance, if only the soul did not conceive iniquity from its pleasure in sin, if only from this conception there did not come forth this wicked birth.

82. Surely if the fear of the Lord kept careful watch it would forthwith deny entrance at the door of the heart to every kind of sin, and just as by its watchfulness it kept sin from entering the soul, so by penitence it would drive from the inner self that which through negligence might have entered. For the fear of God is the lover of innocence and equally a zealous imitator of righteousness, wont to restore lost innocence by the uprightness of righteousness. When the soul which has lost its innocence and wronged God makes satisfaction to God for itself through penitence, does it not seem to you that by its penitence it regains innocence? Was it not more pleasing to innocence not to have gone down from Jerusalem to Jericho, not to have fallen among thieves, than to have

secured remedies for a state of health that had been injured by robbers?* Blessed is he who by repenting the loss of innocence rises again to righteousness. But happier he who is so protected by the fear of God that he scorns to do anything against innocence.

*Cf. Lk 10:30

83. Nothing, therefore, is more blessed than the fear of God. When the soul is firmly anchored by its weight it is not disturbed by vain imaginings amid varying circumstances. While it constantly touches and pricks the heart with duty's goad, it scarcely allows anything but the prick itself or the source of the prick to be remembered. He who as a careful guardian successfully keeps watch at the door of his heart offers to love a place for keeping festival in his inmost being. Holy fear easily blows away vain thoughts from the vicinity of the heart, being intent upon God, and with its desire for the purity set before it, it pursues voluptuous thoughts and routs malicious ones by opposing to them simplicity and goodness. Therefore by a dutiful care for holy fear the attacks of sin are checked, rebellious thoughts subdued, conscience keeps sabbath, love celebrates an inward feast and passes a happier leisure in knowing that the spirit is free to attend to heavenly things.

84. Therefore, dear friend, when such a festival has rejoiced your heart, thanks to the love poured out upon it, think of me as sharing in the inward celebration and do not make the good conferred on you only your own, but in your happiness remember your

friend, still a beggar outside.* I say, break your bread for the beggar and your hungry friend. For in this you will prove yourself truly a friend if you refresh your friend's hunger with your bread. Your bread is Christ, your bread is your charity, your bread is your prayer, your bread is remorse expressed in your tears, by which you wash away not only your own sins but those of your friends. With such breads the holy prophet claims that he is refreshed day and night saying: 'My tears have been my bread day and night.'* Surely the more he was fed by this bread the stronger he became to bear the burden of others. The refreshment of the bread of heaven so strengthens a man's heart that he can himself stand firm amid trials, and he is willing and able to show himself strong in bearing his brethren's burdens.*

*Cf. Lk 16:19ff.

*Ps 42:3

*Cf. Ga 6:2

85. He who feeds upon such bread becomes so strong, is firmly fixed with such weight that frivolous and useless thoughts can—I do not say: not overthrow —scarcely move him. When either by the bread of Scriptures or of tears the soul of him who walks in the Lord's vineyard is sweetly and eagerly refreshed, it is not driven, it is not disturbed by the changing winds of thought. The thoughts themselves, just because they are empty, do not bend away from its stability a soul firmly established through the patient endurance of its accustomed diet. When you have been satisfied with such bread, keep for me at least some of the left-overs so that, refreshed by

it, I may myself continue in my tasks, which you know have increased beyond measure and beyond my strength.

86. For the rest, as regards your soul's sickness, about which you complain in your letters, hasten to flee for refuge to the help and care of him who according to his word came to heal not those who are well but the sick.* He is called Christ for he puts healing ointment upon the wounds of the injured. He is called Jesus for he restores to complete health those anointed by him. I want you to have been entrusted to his own effective medicine. With devotion and humility you pray that for my sickness also there may be the potent medicine of his grace. Further, my son, do not be troublesome to me* nor ask from me anything more. Though I do not propose to reply further to your requests yet I shall not cease to love you truly so long as you abide in the truth. Farewell always in the Lord.

*Cf. Mt 9:12

*Cf. Lk 11:7

LETTER VIII
TO
BROTHER OSMUND,

Brother Adam.

LETTER VIII
87

YOU ARE WILY and you are acting with cunning, for what you fear you cannot obtain by yourself you are asking from me through a go-between. And indeed you have brought between us someone to whom I have not been able on this occasion to refuse what you ask through him. Perhaps at another time, if I could withstand such pressure from him on your behalf, I would act otherwise.

88. Well then, you now have the letter for which you asked. You have also my heart in the tenderness of Jesus Christ. And though I might be glad to be free of writing to you, yet I shall never cease to love you in the Holy Spirit.

89. Oh, if only you would keep the poor little letters of my humble self carefully hidden, and not reveal to other's ears the poverty of my insignificance! If you are forbidden by Scripture to praise a man in his lifetime,* why do you strive to heap praises upon the trifling works of my rusticity, especially since the private conversations of our private love should be

*Si 11:30

hidden from all worldly folk? Holy affection always rejoices in secret discourses. This flame is more easily put out when it is somewhat indiscreetly exposed to the winds.

90. See therefore that what I say or write to you privately out of my great love is not made public by you. Because, as I said, the fire of love grows cold or is extinguished by the blasts of windy praise. Farewell always in the Lord.

LETTER IX
TO
OSMUND,

his beloved brother in Christ,
monk of Mortemer:
brother Adam, humble servant of
the brethren of Perseigne,
to die to sin and to live to virtue
at Mortemer.

LETTER IX
91

I WOULD, MY SON, that *Mare Mortuum* may be for you what the Red Sea was to Israel, so that while a free passage through it is given to you by the leading of grace, the Egyptians with Pharaoh following you may be drowned in it.* Triumphing gloriously over them by the hand of Moses, you are hastening through it towards solitude. You have learned by experience that solitude is the closest friend of the love of God. He who is free to devote himself to the love of heavenly things flees the crowd, avoids noise and with Mary scorns the constant busyness of Martha,* so that he may more surely as more secretly hear and see Christ. Indeed, nothing contributes more to the exercise of love than to be solitary, that is, to be a monk. For the monk's religious and quiet way of life is the very solitude that holy love longs for. Yet the devotion of this love is not founded upon the leisure given by a solitude so complete that it is free from a fear arising from devout concern. But the loving soul is always awe-filled and fearful lest

*Cf. Ex 14:21ff.

*Cf. Lk 10:38-42, Letter V, n. 2

through negligence it should not be occupied in good works to the peril of its love. And such is godly love. But nevertheless brotherly love is full of a tender anxiety and he who sincerely loves another hardly turns his eyes from looking upon the one of whom he is fond.

92. See, my son, I have received your affectionate letters and I have read them, and from the reading I have realized more clearly that love is really never idle. Where it plants its affection, there it directs its gaze and does not allow it to fail to see, with a gaze never satisfied, what it delights to love with constant and eager affection. The saying of the poet seems to discern this, though he speaks of a very different love: 'Love is a thing full of anxious fear.'* As by its nature fire does not cease to draw for its nourishment the fuel placed under it, so the spirit of one who loves, fired by love's longing, draws everything that it loves to the increase of its joy, ponders on it anxiously, speaks of it joyfully, and wherever it has placed the treasure of its affection there it delightedly gathers together the fondness and gaze of its spirit. For where there is love there is the eye, and according to the gospel saying: 'Where your treasure is, there also is your heart.'*

*Ovid, Heroides 1.5.12

*Mt 6:21

93. Everyone has his own joy in his love and he rejoices more fully and meditates with greater delight on the subject about which he is more concerned. My son, what is wonderful in this? Surely

among the soul's powers none is freer than love, none more generous, none sweeter, none equally strong. When that flame has discovered the fuel that suits it it blazes furiously, glows sweetly, warms gently and, when it has thoroughly caught fire, hardly anything quenches it.

94. But you should consider what kindling you bring to your fire. You can very easily be deceived when you love ardently a thing that you have by no means proved by experience to be worthy of your love. Love must be devoted to virtue. Only virtue of soul is to be loved in human beings. But since only virtue of soul is to be sought after, it should be especially and eagerly imitated. It should also be loved single-mindedly in whomsoever it exists.

95. I have spoken this way, my dear friend, because you are too quickly captivated and you seem to love me as if you knew about some sanctity of mine. But although I am happy to be loved, though unworthy, yet I would not have you be deceived in the love of anyone. Love God, the fount of wisdom, the source of virtue, the giver of grace, the guarantee of glory, the dispenser of blessedness. To serve him is to reign; to love him is virtue; to cling to him sanctity, to come to him salvation; to possess him honor and glory; to be with him is blessedness and happiness everlasting.

96. For the rest, as you declare in your letters that you ask nothing from me, you seem to be observing well my prohibition. But, I ask, why do you write to me unless

to ask in return some written reply, with the result that, since I am, as it were, compelled to answer your letters, you seem indirectly to be asking for them. However, I will not for this reason be angry with you if you wish and are able to write more often to me, because truly from frequent correspondence comes proof of an abiding affection.

97. I for my part ask nothing of you except that your prayers should continue to God on behalf of my sins and that by his grace you so live as to be worthy to obtain what you ask. For I have no confidence in my own merits unless another's prayer aids and supports me. Farewell always in the Lord.

LETTER X

TO

ALL THOSE

*who piously venerate
the memory of blessed Martin,**
*Adam, a little one among
his devotees—
keep close to the footsteps
of the same master.†*

**of Tours.*

†*Canon Jean Bouvet, editor of the Latin text, takes exception to the theory of Georges Goyau (Histoire religieuse de la France [Paris, 1942] p. 57) that Adam wrote this letter while he was librarian at Marmoutier at the behest of Guibert of Gembloux. He points out that Guibert was named abbot of Gembloux only in 1194, six months after Adam had assumed the abbatial seat at Perseigne. See SC 66:164-5.*

LETTER X
98

I HEAR THAT A GREAT MANY are scandalized because the church sings and glorifies our Martin as the equal of the Apostles.† This praise of Martin re-echoes on the lips of the church almost throughout the world, most of all in those places where his sanctity is honored frequently and with devotion. Therefore I intend to confute those who are jealous of Martin, to pursue his traducers, praying especially for the grace of help from Him by whom he was found worthy to be called and to be the equal of the apostles. For He who alone is beyond compare and is above all and without equal, whose peace passes all understanding,* was able to make equal to the apostles this man endowed with unique glory, and without doubt did so make him their equal. But those creatures that are far beneath him in so far as the dignity of his nature or the goodness of the Creator has raised him do not draw

*Cf. Ph 4:7

†Cf. The hymns of Odo of Cluny *Rex Christe, Martini decus*, and of Adam of St Victor *Gaude Sion, quae diem recolis*. They refer to Martin as *par* and *compar Apostolis*.

back from sharing an equality with him. And because the Creator's authority has established it, those united in charity bear no grudge. What follows then? Was it possible or not possible that Martin should be the equal of the Apostles? If it was not possible and the omnipotence of God is confined within some sort of limits, how does it happen that in the Scriptures God is called omnipotent? Perhaps God is omnipotent but he was unwilling to bestow the privilege of grace, with which he endowed the apostles, on those who followed them perfectly. But if, as is true, the omnipotent could bring it to pass that they, who by their virtuous life maintained the perfection of the apostles, obtained also equality with them, what prevents Martin from being given the height of apostolic rank? Was it because he did not receive sufficient grace to merit it? Or did he receive it but the jealousy of the apostles (which is sin to utter) denied him a share in their glory? Who would dare even to think this? Perhaps someone says: 'Martin is not the equal of the apostles in glory because he was less than they in sanctity.' How do you prove this, whoever you are who says it? Do you draw your proof from the fact that the apostles were chosen before him, for they were called by the Lord present in the flesh and by him were named 'apostles' as an epithet? If Martin is their inferior because he did not have these advantages, then Paul also is their inferior because he came to the faith later and did not see the Lord in the flesh and did not deserve to be honored by him with the granting of the name 'apostle' as did the others of whom it is written that he named them apostles.* *Cf. Lk 6:13

99. But if you put the apostles before him because they were privileged to see the Lord in person in the flesh before he suffered and after his resurrection when he appeared to them and talked to them, this was given to many others also because as Paul witnesses: 'He was seen by more than five hundred brethren at once.'* Surely Martin gained what we read was granted to no other: the privilege of seeing Christ the Lord before he was born again.* O glorious soldiers–cloak of our catechumen, with which Christ thinks it not shameful to be clothed! But far more glorious was the faith of the one born again to whom Christ denied nothing for which he prayed. *1 Co 15:6 *i.e. baptized

100. For if one argues about miracles and would have the apostles preferred to him in respect of powers, the whole world, bearing witness to Martin, cries out that he, or rather Christ in him, worked more [miracles] than any authentic writer testifies about anyone else. Lastly, if one objects that the sick were placed in Peter's shadow and were healed,* we read too that miracles often came from the straw mat on which Martin lay. It is a greater thing that a cheap mat should work a miracle in Martin's absence than that the shadow of Peter should cure the sick, for this could not happen without Peter being present. *Cf. Ac 5:15

But without Christ, neither Peter present nor Martin absent could work any miracle. These miracles are indeed wonderful and worthy of admiration whether it be the shadow of Peter in his presence or in his absence Martin's pallet, on which he had lain, that worked the wonders.

101. Far more wonderful things have we found and seen in Martin only. Sometimes it happened that while he was hurrying to visit a sick man, before he had completed half the journey, the invalid felt the power of the man approaching and it was a person restored who went forth to meet him. It was sufficient for the restoration to health of a sick man that Martin should not simply have arrived but that he had begun his journey. Sulpicius Severus vouches for this in the case of his uncle Evantius.†

102. In the Apostles' favor perhaps someone puts forward the privilege of martyrdom. Martin was not by the shedding of his blood a martyr, but his whole life was a martyrdom. Both their own wills and the exigencies of the times made the apostles martyrs, but what glory should Martin lose on this account? If the

---

†Sulpicius Severus (+ 591) composed his life of St Martin shortly before the saint's death in 397. This, and his three letters and two dialogues about Martin, form the basic hagiographic sources. The Latin text can be found in *Sulpicii Severi, Libri qui supersunt*, CSEL I (1866) ed. Karl Halm. An English translation of the three, now out of print, was made by F. R. Hoare and published as *The Western Fathers* (London and New York [Sheed and Ward] 1954; New York [Harper Torchbooks] 1965).

exigencies of the times did not offer him the sword of the persecutor, yet the will to suffer was not absent from his heart.† Is the man deprived of the glory of martyrdom who, it is agreed, lived as a martyr in desire? Otherwise the martyr's glory is denied to John the apostle because torture did not deprive him of life, though Truth bears witness that he was going to drink His cup.*

*Cf. Mk 10:35-40, Mt 20:20-23

103. This cup of the passion Martin certainly drank. Through countless crosses of an extraordinary abstinence he voluntarily tortured himself and, as Jesus' unconquered witness in ashes and goat's hair, he gave up his spirit. If therefore Martin, as far as was in him, was a martyr, will the virtue of a most holy will not have the value of the actual deed in the eyes of Him who judges according to intention, especially since the whole merit of a man consists of his good purpose? A man's works are not his merits but the sign of his merits; although even if we were to gather his perfection from his deeds, still no one would come before Martin.

104. But perhaps someone will judge Martin as less than the apostles in that they were princes of the peoples,* teachers of the world, founders and foundations of the church, first tutors of the faithful, in as much as they possess the dignity of the magisterial chair in the school of Christ; wherefore reason does not allow disciples

*Cf. Ps 113:8

†Cf. Sulpicius, Ep 2 to Aurelius CSEL 1:143-4. Antiphon on the Magnificat for second vespers of the Feast of St Martin.

to be equal to their masters, especially since the Master and Lord of all says: 'The disciple is not above the master nor the slave above his lord.'* What follows then? Because the authority of the supreme teacher forbids the disciple to be above his teacher, does it say that he cannot therefore be his equal? Hear what follows: 'It is sufficient,' he says, 'for the disciple to be as his master.'* Notice that equality with a master is not denied to the disciples if the disciple tries to equal the master's perfection by his zeal to imitate him.

*Mt 10:24, cf. Lk 6:40

*Ibid.

105. Therefore Martin was a perfect disciple of the apostles, and in rank an apostolic priest* notable for apostolic deeds, and almost more than an apostle in working miracles. What then prevents him from receiving equal glory when likeness to their lives in all points recommends him? What follows? When we believe or assert these things concerning Martin, do we diminish at all the sublimity of the apostles? Perish the thought! According to our ability we extol the apostles more when we do not deny that it is the imitation of them that becomes Martin's perfection. However, although he is not unequal to them in glory because he was not unequal to them in life, yet the sublimity of the apostles exceeds his to some extent, just as cause goes before effect, as matter before what is made from it, as the origin comes before the things that take their beginning from it. Since there the apostolic teaching is the cause and the matter and the origin

*A bishop

of faith and discipline and reverence in the fathers, for this reason it should and can be set before all other. But it does not for that reason surpass the whole world in merit or glory.

106. On what principle are they not equal to the apostles who lead a life like the apostles, work the same miracles, will pass the same judgements, will rule as they do, and will receive with them the same one penny after the same toil in the same vineyard?* This alone is relevant, that in the payment of the penny the householder has no favorites.* But the last become first and the first last.† Nor is there envy among the recipients nor a boasting about their deserts. Why then do you look askance at Martin's equality with the apostles when there is such integrity in the one who made the payment, such charity among those who received it, that he who was the last to work is found the first in accepting payment. 'The last,' He says, 'shall be first and the first last.'* Is your eye evil because the dispenser of the reward is good,* because the good pleasure of the giver is such that when all are made equal by receiving the same penny, yet the latest are paid before the first? What difference can there be between those to whom the same penny, of equal value, is paid? Surely although there is among the elect unequal renown because star differs from star in glory,* yet in that unequal glory there is an equal joy since God is all in all.† If there is such equality among all the elect,

*Mt 20:1-16

*RB 2:20, 34:2, Cf. Ac 10:34, Jm 2:9

†Cf. Mt 19:30, 20:16, Mk 10:31, Lk 13:30

*Ibid.

*Cf. Mt 20:15

*1 Co 15:41
†Cf. 1 Co 15:28

however much they differ in merit, that there is one and the same joy in the consummation of charity, in the vision of the Creator, in the eternity of immortality, what glory do you think Martin received beyond the rest, he who was beyond all others illuminated with apostolic perfection as he kept close to the footsteps of the apostles by the privilege of his virtues, the power of his miracles?

107. But if the arguments I have traced are not sufficient support for my assertion, finally let one be put forward which makes it clear that Martin did not fall short of the perfection of the apostles. Truly the Holy Spirit was given to the apostles and those who imitated them, but never, or very rarely, did he descend upon any of the saints in the way that he came upon the apostles. But he who appeared upon the apostles visibly in fire* showed himself also in the same form and power in a globe of fire above the head of Martin while he was offering the sacraments.* Although he did not confer upon Martin the gift of tongues because it was not necessary, yet he fired him with such a flame of divine love that even while living in the body he was all aflame through the charity in his heart. And after he left the body he appeared at times visibly all on fire. Hence it comes that he was revealed in fire to Trojanus, holy bishop of Saintes,* and at the funeral of Peleagia, mother of Abbot Aredius, a fiery globe came from heaven lighting up the church, while the possessed

*Cf. Ac 2:3-4

*Sulpicius, Dialogue 2.2; CSEL 1:181-2

*Cf. Gregory of Tours, De gloria confessorum 59; PL 71:870-71

cried out that Martin had come to the obsequies of the departed.* Similarly he appeared to Gregory of Tours as he was bringing his relics into the new basilica.* A certain Brachio also as he entered the oratory was used to seeing a globe of fire running to and fro through the upper parts of the church.*

*Ibid. 104; 903-904B

*Ibid. 20; 842A-44A

*Ibid. 39; 858B, and Vitae patrum 12.3; 1064 A

108. It is not therefore heretical or foolish to acknowledge that a man in all respects apostolic is raised to the fellowship of equality with the apostles. Anyone who through ignorance disparages the merits of Martin should read, mark and learn that the Lord said not only of the apostles but of those who imitate them: 'I will, Father, that where I am there also may my servant be.'* What does 'where I am' mean but that 'such as I am?' [It is] as if he were to say: 'I will that my servants may through grace attain to the glory which by my nature I have.' So it is written: 'When he shall appear we shall be like him for we shall see him as he is.* What follows? Are only the apostles the servants of Christ? Is not Martin also a servant of Christ and the most perfect among the perfect? If therefore the servants of Christ in glory and for this reason equal to him, how can there not be equality among the servants of Christ? But if anyone through envy disparages the claims of Martin, let him be corrected. Martin's God is powerful, working marvels in Martin to avenge his saint and to put an end to such rash assertion, especially since a reverent

*Jn 17:24

*1 Jn 3:2

doubt concerning hidden things is better for you than a quarrelsome argument about uncertainties.

109. Therefore, for the rest, reverence Martin, you who hitherto either through ignorance or through envy had disparaged him. And do not deny that he is equal to the apostles whom you do not doubt to be equal to Christ in glory, if he is seen to speak truth who says: 'We shall be like him for we shall see him as he is.'* Here we need the mediation of Martin that he who is like Christ and therefore deserved to be not unequal to the apostles, by living the apostolic life, by imitating Christ, and by Christ's gift may obtain for us pardon while we still live in the land of unlikeness,† may bring us back to grace, and may bring us into the glory which he has with Christ, from Christ who lives and reigns from age to age. Amen.

*Ibid.

---

†*Regio dissimilitudinis:* a favorite theme among early Cistercians. Bernard, *Sermo* 42 *de diversis* (PL 183:1176), *Gra* 10.32 (OB 3:188), Aelred, *Iesu* 3 (CF 2:6), William, *Med* 4:6 (CF 3:133), *Nat am* (PL 180:401A), *Phys corp* 2 (PL 180:725C). See Etienne Gilson, 'Regio dissimilitudinis de Platon à saint Bernard de Clairvaux,' MS 9 (1947) 108-130, and M. Schmidt, 'Regio dissimilitudinis,' *Freiburger Zeitschrift für Philosophie und Theologie* 15 (1968) 63-108.

LETTER XI
TO
ODO,

venerable Cantor of Bourges,*
whom he loves in the Holy Spirit,
Brother Adam, sinner,
sends greeting.

*Odo (Eudes) of Sully, cantor at Bourges and from 1196-1208 bishop of Paris. This letter seems to have been written in the year of Odo's elevation to the bishopric (1196) — SC 66:181, n. 1. Cf. letter 13, below.

LETTER XI
110

IT HAS OFTEN CROSSED MY MIND, dear friend, to write to you so that you may to some extent know what deep affection I have for you and so that the affection of your love for me may grow warm again. If only my words would take with you the place of oil, by which (when thrown on the flame of your love) the same flame might be fed and increase! I say: fed and increased towards me. Although I am not worthy of your friendship I do not doubt that you love whatsoever things are worthy.

111. Meanwhile my poverty of soul stands in need of no other good and longs for no other profit from the transactions of friendship than to be worthy to love happily and to be loved faithfully. This is the sum total of my commerce with my friends. This is the only subject I have when writing to them, nor can I praise or love in them anything but that which is able firmly to unite us. Happy the unity from whose closeness holy love destroys and disjoins anything that is not separated from worldly

vanity! Happy the love which has its origin in virtue and has no incentive other than the works of truth! Happy the love, I say, whose foe is worldly hope, whose whole aim lives in longing for what is eternal! Surely according as holy love is impatient of corruption, so also it is suspicious of anything it knows to be subject to vanity. Finally, as it does not lack a vigorous striving for improvement, so it does not lack the realization of what should be striven for, so it is not deceived. So it learns about the splendor of truth lest the manifold vanities of dark inconstancy should blind it. When virtue is fully occupied, love is fired with longing for incorruption and exerts itself to prevent the desire of the flesh from rendering it soft and nerveless.

112. If to such progress is added perseverance, what reward will holy love achieve when made perfect? What glory will it have when the truth shines forth in full splendor? What sweetness and charm will it have when by its longing for unfailing virtue it glows in the noonday of love complete? O blessed anticipation! O reward towards which all vows should strive. Happy the soul that when it has found this pearl* does not delay selling bit by bit everything that by comparison is alien to it. Therefore the ownership of body and of soul must be unhesitatingly set aside so that you may be able to search for the treasure hid in the field* and dig more vigorously, discover it more surely, hold it more firmly,

*Cf. Mt 13:45-46

*Mt 13:44

possess it more joyfully. The burdens of the world are to be cast off, its honors accounted as nothing, all evil driven from the mind, so that to some degree it can taste the first-fruits of holy love. For as it courteously flows into the minds that are pure, so it longs also to find them free, so that the din of earthly activity may not disturb or take possession of them.

113. When the solemn Sabbath of the Holy Spirit is celebrated there is need of a mind at leisure, one which will not to any extent cloud the joy of spiritual holiday with the unseemliness of slavish work. In relaxation from fear the love of wisdom at the beginning takes its rise, putting an end to the disturbance of sin. In the feria of devotion the aim is to be sincerely turned to the worship of God and by tender compassion to give help to the sorrows of the oppressed. In the feria named 'the spirit of knowledge' the soul withdraws into itself, weighs carefully judgement based on its own reason, lest it be blinded regarding its duties through the dimming or cooling of its own small fire. In the feria of fortitude care is taken that when the time of temptation assails, the soul, protected by essential safeguards, may manfully resist. A happy feria is celebrated in the spirit of counsel; the soul, with no confidence in itself, seeks the counsel of the Holy Spirit regarding all its purposes and in the same Spirit spends itself for others as a trusty counsellor in all things. In the feria of understanding there is a celebration of such purity that not

only do earthly affections prove burdensome to the soul, but thoughts of material things do not even enter it, and the more clearly heavenly things are contemplated, the more happily earthly ones are meanwhile not remembered. What shall I say of the last and highest feria which is called the 'spirit of wisdom'? It has not been granted me to know by experience how great is the multitude of joys of this sabbath. For I have not yet deserved to celebrate the foregoing ferias. If I have not yet, in the spirit of the fear of the Lord, said farewell to the slavery of sin and the disturbances of vice, how should I dare to discuss the other ferias of wisdom or the very sabbath of wisdom?

114. From this very audacity it is easy to understand that I have not yet received the spirit of understanding and wisdom, in that I have dared in my inexperience to discuss matters so recondite. Yet I trust that in the eyes of a friend love will excuse my baldness. Holy friendship has this duty: that while in the case of a fault it in no wise covers up the fault, yet it does not refuse to grant forgiveness with a generous readiness to the person who acknowledges it. Truly if the spirit of the fear of the Lord were in me, I should have been afraid either to be or to seem boastful and I would rather hide myself under a peck of humility than tread among things too great and wonderful for me.

115. All presumption is hateful to holy humility and no matter what heights

humility has reached it considers nothing safer for itself than prudent concealment. It gazes eagerly at heaven, while in accordance with the significance of its name it does not separate itself from the earth, and the lower it sinks in its own estimation the more the height of heavenly matters inclines towards it. Somehow also the voluntary depression of humility avails to bend the heavens and with wondrous ease it reaches a heavenly height, at the same time gladly staying on the earth, and desiring nothing from the earth it prides itself only on the witness of conscience. Far, far different is that pride, born on high, which strives, according to the meaning of its name, to pass above itself and to overtop itself, and having fallen headlong through its own weight, is shattered and broken beyond repair.

116. Every loftiness, therefore, is to humility suspect, for she knows it to be the friend of pride. Whatever the flesh considers glory humility hates and abominates, though in her simplicity she so controls herself that she neither wishes nor dares to pass judgment in any matter. Loving silence, seeking the hidden, she confines herself within the limits of her own insignificance so that she has no other aim than to know herself. She believes it unnecessary to know anything else and thinks it vanity to be known by others. She is free from excess as she is free from boasting, in the case of the one exercising temperance and in the other being on fire with the desire for justice.

Here you may see the great prudence of humility which fortifies the citadel of the soul with these defences, while its firmness of purpose renders it impregnable in every onslaught.

117. O happy, truly essential virtue of humility. It desires nothing but to know itself, but the treasure of heavenly wisdom is not hidden from its understanding. For beneath the thought of its own worthlessness the humble soul conceals the fire of a secret love, as it were beneath ashes, and from it the smithy of a devout heart is kindled to give light and heat. How gladly the humble Christ betakes himself to such a lodging, where a careful humility keeps the fire of love always ready for his coming. As the psalmist says: 'A fire shall go before him,'* and to receive him is that soul which needs not beg fire or oil from among strangers. These come from within and from heaven, and he who has willed that the fire once kindled within him should last carefully bars all entrances through which the lightness of a gusty vanity might be able to blow and put out the fire. But although the fire which has been raging fiercely is not extinguished by the wind that blows, but burns the more, yet humility is so full of fear that it never thinks it safe to go forth from the dwelling of a lowly conscience. There it freely contemplates Mary, star of the sea,* there it assists joyfully at the virgin's childbearing, there it attaches itself wholly to the cradle of the Word, shares in the play of infancy—

*Ps 97:3

*Cf. Hymn Ave maris stella from the office of BVM on Saturday.

thanks to the happy innocence of its life—and in exultation of heart prattles with him with devout cries. Humility counts as precious silks those little bands in which the infant Word is swaddled. Then it turns with all eagerness to the divine shrine of the holy breast and as far as leisure allows sucks the heaven-filled breasts.*

*Cf. Antiphon Nesciens mater, above, Lr 3, p. 77.

118. With such nourishment meanwhile is the tender infancy delighted, so that when, as age advances, it arrives at perfect manhood, it can take up and accomplish the task of the cross. This is a task for the fully grown. Their age, more advanced in the virtue which keeps their faculties trained through constant use,* has by the study of wisdom given them their beards. My Jesus deals well with me if he counts me among those suckled with him, if at times he receives me and shares with me at his mother's breast the tiny drops of soothing liquid. For this Word of the Father, the bread of life, willed to be made small in the milk of the flesh so that he who in the form of God was the solid food* of angels might by the limitation of his incarnation empty himself* to become a tiny mouthful for little ones.

*Cf. Heb 5:14

*Cf. Heb 5:13-14

*Cf. Ph 2:7

119. I beseech you, dear friend, when you have tasted the banquet of a more nourishing food, when the food of the fullgrown has delighted you, do not be unmindful of me. If sometimes at the moving of the Holy Spirit you have attained to the sabbath of wisdom, make this at least your prayer for me, that I be not expelled from

the dwelling place of the infant Word. Meanwhile here is the whole ground of my philosophy, nowhere but here could I be with greater pleasure; on this hangs all my hope and expectation. I am a little child who needs milk not solid food* and yet whatever my friends' blessed hunger for more solid food consumes, I do not doubt turns to my profit.

*Cf. Heb 5:13-14

120. However, dear friend, I shall see you face to face when there is leisure, since in the meantime there is as yet none. The poor harvest of this current year and the ruin the whole world shares are keeping me at home and compelling me, as it were, to attend a kind of funeral. I shall however go out someday, God willing, from this tomb and be brought to life in seeing and talking with my friends. Meanwhile you will greet in my name those who you have found love me with true charity. I thank you for your generosity on behalf of those two poor little women, God fearing as I believe, for whom in this time of famine you in your pity for the most part provided at Bagneaux. I pray you not to let your pity withdraw its hand from them. The exigency of hunger has not yet been withdrawn from them. Farewell.

LETTER XII
TO
HIS FATHER,

*and dear friend in Christ,
brother Adam his humble son:
may he be restrained
from the desires of the flesh
by the prison of Christ.* *

*Letter to H, his father and dear friend — Douai MS 374 identifies an H who had asked to be received at Perseigne. Reference to 'my father' and 'your holiness' may indicate that the recipient was a bishop, perhaps Hamelin of Le Mans. (Cf. Letter 54).

LETTER XII
122

My father, I owe myself wholly to your humility, and would that I had as great an opportunity for obedience as I have the will to obey. But as it is, the impossibility which brings shame upon my will brings also this, that my friend suffers refusal of his request. The unwonted barrenness of this year forces me to wean my little ones and compels me, not without great grief of heart, to transfer them to nourishment provided by other houses. So meanwhile, in the absence of the community, it is permitted to receive no one, especially since without the council of our brethren we should not venture anything of this kind.* Your discernment will readily accept the excuse, and between true friends true affection does not pretend that something due to inability is a failure of duty.

123. But my love for you as a son invites me to inquire about the state of your holiness. And would that I could get to know more often of your circumstances. I should call you completely happy, for

*Cf. RB 3

solitude with Christ is so congenial to you that anything that tastes sweet in Egypt disgusts you. Happy the one to whom the world's delight has brought loathing, who has despised the mud and the bricks of Pharaoh and treated with contempt the dung pit of Babylon, when comparing it with the gold of Jerusalem. How happy is the anticipation of him who has brought himself to the study of virtue, for whom Christ alone is desirable, upon whom the brightness of blessed immortality has already shone. I have no doubts about you, that the love of Christ holds you close, and whatever collapse of temporal things you have experienced, the steady purpose of your heart will remain firm through your love of that which endures. Narrow is the way of righteousness and hard but to those who despise the world, the gentle unction flowing into the heart from the sweetness of the Holy Spirit lightens it. Make me, I beg you, a sharer in your experience of this. Although because of difficulties I do not grant your request, yet do I not cease to love sincerely the prisoner of Christ. Farewell.

LETTER XIII
TO
ODO,

his dear father in Christ,
by the grace of God,
Bishop of Paris*
Brother Adam, least of all monks,
gives greeting in the spirit
of knowledge and piety.

*Cf. Lr XI.

LETTER XIII
124

AS OFTEN AS MY FRIEND WRITES, my understanding of friendship and my experience of a longstanding love come back to my memory. I confess, reverend Father, that my affection does not feel you to be in harmony with itself in the way it was previously used to feeling. But I would rather attribute this not to the friend's wrongdoing but rather to a faulty affection, though something presents itself to my mind as the reason why the affection seems, not without justification, to have changed.

125. Indeed through changing circumstances the nature of love varies and in the face of differing situations and differing circumstances it is wont to fluctuate. When therefore in one and the same man I consider the friend and the bishop, and the one rejoices in the familiar warm regard while the other demands reverence for his high office, love that knows nothing of reverence and will not brook lordship, does not harmonize with such a difference. When an

obligation to reverence intervenes in a matter of love, love suffers loss because of the difference in rank, and charity complains that it is deprived of its right when it is exiled from the fellowship of unity. While, therefore, due reverence is paid to preferment, affection that knows nothing of compulsion is driven to leave the confines of a mutual union and without doubt the warmth of feeling diminishes. On this account it becomes slower to make visits, more reserved in conversation, more bashful in giving greeting, more timid in making requests, more niggardly in giving. Since therefore I am the least among mere ordinary folk while you are great among the most illustrious, what agreement, I ask, can there be in circumstances so different, to make friendship delight in the equality it loves when the situations are so dissimiliar?

126. I have not spoken thus, reverend Father, because I shall one day cease to respect and love you, not as long as virtue and truth continue to dwell with you. To love these, to whatever undertaking they come, is my unqualified purpose, Jesus being my helper. Nor shall I be able to fail a person whom grace has willed to illuminate with such splendor. Though freely-given love generally views with suspicion any compulsion towards reverence, yet the lover of virtue cannot fail to love it even in bishops—though it strives to restrain its feeling lest by its action it should betray itself outwardly.

127. The approbation given by

despicable men to those in public view is easily shown in a crowd, and so the purity of love is more wisely kept within the bounds of feeling than revealed outwardly by clear signs. I, therefore, who live in the cloister have chosen with more pleasure and greater safety to visit the hut of a Cistercian philosopher than to follow my friend and visit him in city after city, the friend whom I grieve almost to have lost in the bishop. Yet I receive a pleasant recompense for this loss if through your reverence pity and truth accomplish among others—and especially among those under you—what they have laid upon you to do through your priestly office. You are a pillar of salt:* show yourself available to all for the feeding and profit of your beasts, so that you who have been raised above the height of the candlesticks may blaze out as a lantern for all.

*Cf. Gn 19:26, Mt 5:13

128. The time has come for the brightness of your glory to shine forth more clearly since that star of the morning has set from the firmament of the church. By the bright rays of his life and the brilliance of his doctrine he so often shed light upon our hemisphere. I think you know, for I am speaking to a wise man, that I have been speaking of the Canon of Paris of pious memory. I would that you were grieving for the death of such a great man, but in the opinion of certain men you did not sorrow at all at his absence; yet I could not give credence to this.

129. Meanwhile let us pass over other

things which the opinion of the common herd lays against your reputation, though they would deserve a harsher invective if there were some who truly loved you, who finding them to be true were to find you open to that friend's correction.

130. Perhaps you plead that I speak disrespectfully and in speaking so boldly against a bishop am not sensible of humility. But this is just what I said before, that love knows nothing of respect. Furthermore, just as the mind talks to itself, so it speaks with a friend fearlessly. I confess, I have forgotten the reverence due to a bishop because I still keep something of my old affection and though I am absent I shall never be able to spare you. Whatever respect may be due to your office, your faults should have reproof, your virtues love. I pray that our zeal may not find in a friend cause for suffering or inflicting a wound, but rather what gives joy and delight.

131. However, when I have won the privilege of seeing your Paternity, I shall express to you in speech what I have at present thought better to be silent upon. Yet I do not think I ought to pass over in silence what has been spread abroad by general rumor, namely, that you have taxed the priests of your diocese, a course which seems far removed not only from perfection but also from piety and justice. By this, venerable Father, you have produced a serious stumbling-block for those who love you, and those who were looking

for a flame rather than smoke from the lantern placed above the candelabrum are surprised and grieved that you are smoking rather than flaming. Smoke is always troublesome to eyes and nostrils and those who hoped to see from you examples of light and to catch the scent of a good hope are on both accounts suffering vexation from their opposites.

132. What is more staunch than true friendship? What more genuine than a charity that is steadfast? It does not doubt that from a bit of leaven the whole lump is corrupted.* Yet it does not allow the conscience to be branded by any evil which can be avoided. May you not let that evil action become habitual nor let the unhappy world be brought by your example to follow it, but rather by the medicine of an obvious repentance teach that they should not do the thing which you have taught them by your example is not blameworthy. So great a bishop, so longed-for by everyone, so prayed for in the devout prayers of all the saints, so bedewed with the tears of the faithful in order to bring forth the seeds of perfection, ought not to have on his conscience, much less do openly, what harms his reputation and cheats the devout expectations of everyone.

133. But if, as some assert, when you were burdened with many debts, sheer necessity compelled you to take action, but where no tyrannical extortion or coerced exaction was involved but where a humble and suppliant pleading of necessity

*Cf. 1 Co 5:6, Ga 5:9

would have made a kindly request, I should certainly call this not so much a tax as a contribution. Though this does not reek of perfection, yet it was better to do this once in a lifetime than at the crippling moment of uncertain death to leave debts unpaid, to the great danger of the debtor and irreparable loss to the creditor. Very often, indeed almost always, it happens to bishops as they are dying to be so stripped of their possessions by the secular power that what they owe or what they bequeath cannot be paid.

134. Charity usually puts the better construction on doubtful matters. Reflect, for your part, what your conscience says on this matter, lest avarice, the servitor of idols,* should make of a christian bishop an idol worshipper.

*Cf. Ep 5:5, Col 3:5

135. Even if your heart does not rebuke you, yet what looks like evil has been committed to the scandal of all men, and an opportunity is given malicious persons to revile you, while the well-disposed grieve that they are losing what they hoped for in you. For the rest, Father, I keep in my heart feelings which it would be tedious and perhaps unworthy to write. When our messenger or messengers have revealed them to your reverence by word of mouth, if you consider them worth your attention, I humbly and earnestly ask you to carry them out.

LETTER XIV
TO
MASTER B.,

Canon of Paris,*
my dear friend in Christ.

*Master B. has not been identified.

LETTER XIV
136

APPLY YOURSELF TO THE MATTERS which you need to try out. For many act otherwise and give their wholehearted attention to pursuits which necessity does not demand nor the concern for truth require. Indeed, those activities should be pursued and deserve the approval of good men which virtue commends, a pure conscience perfects, the brightness of truth illuminates, and the excellence of true charity sets its mark upon.

137. My dear son, I am filled with astonishment at your judgment, in that you praise and extol so highly as regards all these considerations my insignificant little writings, which in my opinion seem unworthy of such commendation. The account of a certain monk of ours whom your friendship introduced to the Parisians made it quite clear to me that you praise my letters more generously than is fitting. But though I do not doubt that you do this out of your great love for me, yet I wish that you would praise with greater restraint works which my rustic simplicity dared to

publish under pressure from some individuals.

138. I thought myself a simple countryman, and so far this opinion has not deserted me; but now other men's judgment compels me to believe about myself something other than I really feel. Now therefore, placed in a dilemma I am not at all sure what to choose: whether to admit the witness of my own conscience concerning myself, or, rejecting the inward witness, to believe the statements of others. It is obdurate and ignorant to believe that so many wise men can be mistaken in their judgment. Nevertheless it is foolish for me to think of myself as different from what my conscience tells me. However, it is safer for every man to follow the judgment of his own heart about himself than to be foolishly puffed up by the witness of another man's talk.

139. For the rest, dear friend as you show plainly that you try to obtain my writings, you still continue to ask and do not cease to urge me to write for you something about the sins with which the whole human race is palpably and almost incurably ensnared. And in asking this you have driven to discuss and treat of sins a man who has been used to nothing else but to be moved by sins and to commit them.

140. Experience of vices has taught me to discuss vice inasmuch as the perversity of corrupt conduct has always shown me to be sinful. If you had asked a vice-ridden man to discuss the virtues you would have

incurred the ridicule of angels and men. For since virtue is the soul's health and vice its sickness, how shall a sick man lecture about health and a sinful man about virtue? I do not say that a resolution to attain to virtue has not flashed upon me, with grace to help me. But long-standing feebleness, grown serious through the experience of vice, does not yet allow me to know what virtue is. The heat of a deep-seated fever has indeed cooled down under Christ's care, since through the medicine of his grace the resolution toward sin has ceased, but still lying, as it were, upon my bed, I have not regained full-strength nor have I been able to regain an appetite for the food which is essential. For I should say that the essential food is a longing for virtue and the hunger and thirst for righteousness.* Those who hunger for restoration by this food are seen to have recovered from their illness. But those who wallow in their vices grow sick until their salvation is imperiled. And not only do they feel the desires of the flesh active within them, but they give consent and what was vice in thought through that consent is brought to completion in sin. Therefore the feebleness of nature affects the mind beyond measure and against reason, and through consent breaks forth into action.

*Cf. Mt 5:6

141. Consent is the spontaneous acquiescence of the will which fans the tinder of vice and becomes the seedbed of evil action. Hence now in lovers of the world, in the sons of darkness, are manifest

the deeds of the flesh, which are fornication, uncleanness, the worship of idols, and similar sins mentioned by the Apostle.* *Ga 5:19

142. Among other plagues of these vices, fleshly indulgence is as conspicuous as it is menacing. As long as in its nature it is possessed as it were of a corrupt body, it can less easily be avoided. Yet this is possible through the help of grace. The disease of incontinence existing in the flesh that is dead through sin is either saved from collapsing into degrading activity through honorable marriage, or the flesh is so subdued by its striving towards continence that the disease dies, overpowered by mortifications. But those who follow neither course are given over to shamelessness or uncleanness and they display in their persons not only filth of the flesh but, according to the saying of truth, they sin against their own body. For every sin, says Truth, which man has committed is apart from the body but he who commits fornication sins against his own body.* In the case of *1 Co 6:18 other sins he employs the help of his body, but in fornication the whole action involves the body and is in the body so that in this foul work the very essence of the body is defiled. Yet I do not say that only the body's essence is polluted in the sense of meaning to except the soul, to which rather every sin is known to belong. Realize the foulness of the actual deed which brings the body under a degrading yoke of wrongdoing.

143. How far removed is the cheapness

of this filthy activity from the purity and glory of our Lady Virgin! Rather, how entirely distant from the fruit and worth of the virgin birth is he who subjects himself to such baseness. For since our Lady's Son reveals himself only to those who are continent, those who are given over to the lures of the flesh may obviously be considered strangers to the splendors of such great glory. What thing that is clean can they offer to the angelic purity, men who it is agreed are foul and stinking through the contagion of their leprosy; mules who rot in their own dung,* how can they rise to human deeds or the praises of God?

*Jl 1:17 (Vulg.)

144. Human action is rational, and to act irrationally is attributed not to a human being but to a beast. Clearly the foolish beast cannot perform human acts because, while reason is implanted in man, the beast is ignorant of reason. Therefore I say that he who uses not reason, or misuses the reason implanted in him, is called in the judgment of Holy Scripture not man but beast. Hence it follows that it calls men who spend and end their lives in the foulness of luxury 'beasts who rot in their own dung.'* In another place also the Holy Spirit forbids animal wantonness in men: 'Do not,' he says 'become like horse and mule which have no understanding.'* He who puts behind him the law of divine justice after the fashion of beasts and serves his desire instead of living honorably and paying homage to the ever-present deity clearly shows himself to be without

*Ibid.

*Ps 32:9

reason and understanding. Surely when the author and lover of purity is acknowledged with faith unfeigned to be present, the christian would not commit base deeds unless he became a beast.

145. Though he behaves as a beast he is not, however, a beast by nature, but in some fashion he sheds his manhood when in his conduct he loses the use of reason. For although he is superior through the innate gift of reason, and yet he does not consider by whom and in what sort he was created nor understand for what purpose he has received the gift of reason but either does not use it or misuses it, he is justly compared to foolish beasts and becomes like them,* if he is not, as usually happens, found worse than they. For beasts behave according to a blind natural instinct and do not in any way recoil from what has been ordained for them by nature. But man, whose nature it is to reason and understand, abuses the reason implanted in him, he transgresses the commands of divine law, and though he is wretched and powerless he fights against the order set before him by God's ordinances. Man therefore, though he is better than the beasts through the dignity of his nature, is nevertheless by the foulness of his conduct more worthless than they, by his habits more corrupt, by his actions more evil, by his spirit more headstrong, by his physical senses more feeble, to his nature a greater enemy, by ill will more dangerous, by sins more unhappy, and by his expectation of eternal

*Cf. Ps 49:12 & 20. Cf. Bernard, Ann 7; Pl 183: 386C

death more wretched. And in some strange way, thanks to his own malice, he subdues almost everything to himself, under whose feet the goodness of the Creator put all things. 'All things,' he says 'you have put in subjection under his feet,'* but now he laments that he has been made lower than the gnats, for while behaving irrationally, stripping himself of human dignity, he degenerates into a beast not because of his nature but because of his character.

*Ps 8:6

146. Are they not beasts, not so much by folly as by madness, they whom the frenzy of desire befouls with open adulteries, who because they whinny after their neighbor's wife in the fields of untamed license receive in the holy writings the name 'stallions'. Each one, says the prophet, whinnies after his neighbor's wife.* Oh hateful bane of adulterers. If they had not withdrawn their souls from the spotless nuptial couch of Christ, souls with which Christ, in the marriage chamber of the church and on the bed of the cross, had entered upon an alliance of incorrupt wedlock, they would never have handed them over to the brothels of the devil, the corruptor of souls. Are the devil's brothels not the bodies of fornicators, in which insatiable desire eats up all simplicity and honor as a wolf devours a sheep. Yet these bodies Christ dedicated to be his temples by the sacrifice of his own body. Is it a trivial sin or a pardonable offence that the soul should turn to the harlot, that soul for the winning of which as his spouse the

*Jr 5:8

son of eternal virginity has done so much? O wondrous condescension of the zealous lover who did not hesitate to destroy himself in his ardent love for love of the lost soul. He lost his own soul for my sake, as if he could not find mine unless he lost his own through his unspeakable regard for most unworthy me. What then are you doing, shameless harlot? And with what effrontery have you changed the temple of Christ, the marriage chamber of your spouse, into a brothel of Priapus?* Why, ravening wolf, have you by the curse of your desire dedicated to be a brothel of Venus* the dwelling of your body which the passion of Christ had made and consecrated to be a temple for himself. Surely the temple of Christ ought not to be given up to obscene uses, and what was made for the service of heaven the harlot's shamelessness ought not to profane.

*god of procreation

*goddess of love

147. The soul that sins is without a doubt a shameless harlot who inwardly disdains the embraces and kisses of its spotless spouse and through the door of the senses leaps forth to the allurements of voluptuousness. And prostituting herself to the desire of the flesh, to the desire of the eyes, and to the lascivious harlot of the pride of life,* what other than her own body is she exposing in the brothel of fornication? Now henceforth what crime, what disgraceful deed would she hesitate to commit, she who was not afraid to commit that first adultery, that is, to insult heaven and to withdraw from Christ's embrace? From this the harlot falls

*1 Jn 2:16

headlong into every shameful deed, hastens to corrupt and to be corrupted, observes no limit in evil but seeks even more luxury than the flesh subjected to it can provide. Wretched men seek stimulants for their passions and that which accursed nature does not of itself provide to satisfy them artful curiosity and excessive food and drink call forth and inflame to this end.

148. What unhappy times ours are! In them almost the whole body of the world is seen to have befouled itself with luxury so that each sex and age and rank seems soiled with the spots of this evil. Yet hitherto a suitable medicine could have come to the aid of this disease if it had not itself changed into deadly poison by unfortunate intercourse with it. What is meant by: 'even in the angels themselves we have found faults.'* Are they not angels who style themselves clergy, who profess themselves ministers of the church? Are they not angels who have as their duty to stand before the king of angels to proclaim heavenly things to the peoples who stand below them? If the angels are called messengers and the church heaven, what are they who in the church either administer the sacraments or proclaim heavenly teaching to the nations but angels performing their ministry in heaven? Hence it is that in Malachi the priest is called the angel of the Lord of hosts.* And the Apostle orders women to pray in church with heads covered because of the angels,* that is, lest Satan tempt the ministers by their

*Jb 4:18

*Ml 2:7

*1 Co 11:10

nudity. There the ministers of the church are called angels, and to them it is signified that they ought not to gaze upon women, who are bidden to have their heads covered on account of the angels. But if it is lawful for them to see women, how much more unlawful is it for those who wish to seek them or be sought, those on whom pre-eminence of office and the privilege of messenger confer the name angels. But alas, it goes otherwise, for after a fashion not so much notable as notorious the angels of light have been transformed into angels of Satan. And when, on the other hand, according to the apostle it happens that an angel of Satan transforms himself into an angel of light,* the ministers of the church who ought to have been preeminent in all holiness and justice are nowadays not ashamed to become more robust in crime than others who are worldlings. They are not afraid to use the freedom given them as a cloak for malice* nor are they ashamed to submit themselves to the slavery of sin. Nowadays those who ought to have been students of heavenly doctrine have become notorious for their crimes and, owing to their examples, there has grown up a school of vice which ought to have been a school of virtue.

*Cf. 2 Co 11:14

*1 P 2:16

149. If your reflection should wish to consider every vice you will be hard pressed to find a single one of which the clergy have not had not only full experience but complete mastery of it. If it is a question of pride, they are so full of overweeningness

and arrogance that, despising the supreme good, disregarding the eternal good, they glory only in a display of their wealth, the elegance of their dress, and the acquisition of honors. If one treats of envy, it must be that they waste away through the spirit of envy because the desire of the eyes and the pride of life render them utterly devoid of charity.* If you turn your glance towards the frenzy of anger you will see more clearly that there is in them a spirit the more frenzied as it becomes the fiercer because of the preeminence that their proud superiority gives them. For the ferocity of their excitement makes savage and violent those who are not moved by the kindliness of pity. See whether they are conspicuous for *accidie* who are saddened almost beyond consolation at every misfortune, unable to bear even for a short time the loss of their comfortable existence.

*1 Jn 2:15-16

150. What shall we say about avarice, which is called by the apostle the service of idols,* and by which men of this kind clearly confess paganism rather than Christ. For if avarice according to the teaching of Paul is idolatry, what but worshippers of idols shall we call those who we see have preferred to the poverty of Christ and his worship, riches and honors? With them what is there from the patrimony of the Crucified that is not put up for sale; with them profit is held to be piety. Is it not paganism, that is idolatry, to buy an estate or to make ready five yoke of oxen and on

*Ga 5:20, Eph 5:5

those grounds to excuse themselves from the heavenly marriage?* If an estate is called a *pagus** and he who is a pagan† is ready to serve idols, on what principle do those who through avarice, that is the service of idols, not lose the freedom and glory of the name 'christian'? I ask you, by what right do the worshippers of idols claim the inheritance of the Crucified? Those whom the service of idols, that is avarice, draws away from the divine marriage, what right have they in the church's sacraments? Are the sacraments of the church not the dishes of the heavenly marriage feast, which those alone are worthy to enjoy and be refreshed by who come to the wedding and enter with the wedding garment?* See, as intercessors for men avarice has set up Gehazi† and Simon Magus,* who surely neither baptize children nor bury the dead, nor is it through them that the host of salvation is offered for the departed, unless they are hired at an set fee. For this reason they demand 'thirtieths', exact annates, and scarcely anything of their ministry do they perform for free and they have received from their predecessors nothing without payment.

*Cf. Lk 14:15-24
*a country district
†originally, a country dweller

*Cf. Mt 22:1-14
†2 K 5:20-27
*Ac 8:9-24

151. Whether they wish it or not, the faithful of the church are compelled to make as their intercessors with God men whom they clearly know to be given over idolatry and to be established through their despicable life as enemies of God. What does receiving the offerings of the

faithful imply but the obligation to obtain their pardon by prayer? How shall he who takes or demands offerings in affront to [divine] majesty, himself unfaithful, obtain pardon for the faithful? How, I say, would the intercession of a man whose presence is an insult to the divine majesty bring God near to a penitent? 'And when,' Isaiah says, 'you stretch out your hands, I will turn away my face from you and when you multiply your prayers I will not listen to them. Your first days and your solemn festivals my soul hates. Your deeds are grievous to me, I cannot bear them.'* If therefore the presence of such men is grievous in God's sight, how can those who are guilty be purified by the prayers of abandoned men?

152. Clearly we must think differently about the sacrifice of the Mediator lest the saving victim be deprived of his efficacy. As often as it is offered, even by the hands of however unworthy a priest, the victim is rightly called saving, because there is no salvation except in him, and though there is no merit in the celebrant yet by the word of God the sacrament is accomplished and he who celebrates it is made its instrument. But will a man be able to make peace for me with my God who does almost nothing but provoke him to anger? To live by sacrilege, to live by plunder, to be intent upon taxes, to devour the people of God, not to feed them, not to edify their souls but to destroy them, not to correct their morals but to corrupt them, to seek for the sacred

*Is 1:14-15 (inverted)

ministry not honor but censure, and under cover of their holy order and the prayers of the church to give their thoughts to fleshly gain, to make the shadow of liberty the cloak for malice* and for unlawful conduct, what is this but to provoke God to anger?

*1 P 2:16

153. I have mentioned some things but I have passed over many which in the clergy of our times are seen more clearly than daylight, and in a strange fashion those who ought to have been medicine for our dying epoch have instead become its destruction. What should I say about the gluttony of the very men who just as they obviously serve idols through their avarice, also make their belly their God through the vice of gluttony. Hence the saying of the apostle speaking of such men: 'Whose God is their belly and their glory,' he says, 'is in their own shame, who occupy their minds with earthly matters.'* This God they certainly worship with great zeal, offering to him sacrifices as many as the dishes they set before their fellow guests. These men, thanks to these dishes, are more unbridled and more vigorous in the work of Venus, for they are completely at leisure and abound in riches; the more generously the Crucified has entrusted to them the patrimony of the poor, the more self-indulgently they coddle their bodies. As for the rest of men, the slenderness of their resources or the unremitting toil of their tasks occupies them and weakens them, and these things to some extent hold them

*Ph 3:19

back from the enticements of pandering pleasures. But in those who are not engaged in human labors it seems that iniquity comes forth from their grossness* and the poverty of Christ by the harvest of the cross supplies them with complete abundance. But although the father of the poor did not bequeath his patrimony to them to dissipate but to administer faithfully, yet he does not immediately refuse to yield its possession into the hands of guilty men.* Oh, if the stewards of the church would consider for whom, how much, and in what manner the Lamb, the restorer of innocence, labored! For whom did he labor if not for the poor? It was not enough for him to love them unless, emptying himself* he should become one with their poverty by being in the likeness of their flesh. Indeed so far did he honor the wretchedness of his poor by being a companion in their destitution that, while the foxes have holes and the birds of the air their nests, the Lord of heaven and earth has among men no place to lay his head; of this he himself bore witness saying: 'the foxes have holes and the birds of the air their nests but the son of man has no place to lay his head.'* As for his not having labored! All who pass along the way would take note if they turned the gaze of an attentive mind upon him, if only they looked not cursorily or superficially on him in his griefs. Indeed from the sole of his foot to his head* there was in the body of the Lamb not one spot remaining free

*Cf. Ps 73:7

*Cf. Collect for Triduum. See letter 3, above, p. 82

*Cf. Ph 2:7

*Mt 8:20, Lk 9:58

*Is 1:6

from pain. When death seizes his whole body, a death more cruel than any death, what either in his feeling or limbs can remain free from the experience of pain? Consider death's cruelty in his dying body: the kind of cruelty; how undeservedly he endures everything, how he bears it all at the hands of unworthy men. Truly that head which the Baptist fears to touch* is pierced by a thorny crown approved by thorny hearts. But alas! The thorn bush of our sins has produced these thorns and the guilt of our wickedness has provided the means for the affliction of innocence.

*Cf. Antiphon for Terce within the Octave of Epiphany, Brev. cist.

154. That blessed face is struck with the palms of the hands, the face on which the angel's purity delights to gaze is worn out with spitting. Those eyes full of pity and of light the suns of darkness cover and hailing him with derision those who struck him invite him to prophesy.* They are not afraid to make him in his thirst drink from the vinegar and gall of their own bitterness, while they ought eagerly to have drunk from the torrent of his desire the waters of salvation. Those generous hands which with glorious liberality fill all things with blessing* they fastened with nails to a log of wood. But could those hands be so bound and so held by the sons of avarice that they could not bestow the riches of goodness and grace upon the whole creation, especially since the whole world waits for food to be given by him in due season?* May this never be! The Lord is gentle to all and his goodness does not refuse itself to

*Cf. Lk 22:63-4, Mt 26:67, Mk 14:65

*Cf. Ps 145:16

*Cf. Ps 104:27

any man, for he prays for pardon even for those who crucified him and pleads their ignorance to his Father, saying: 'Father forgive them for they know not what they do.'* O wondrous goodness, measureless sweetness, infinite charity! The divine innocence suffers every wrong and in all that he endured he not only overcame the malice of his persecutors but expended upon those who did not deserve it the fullness of his pity. Those blessed feet which did not slip or run into evil received the nails which held them fast. But can the living Word of God, so potent and swift-running, be hindered by these fetters until the course of the obedience which he had set before him cannot be completed? This too be far from us! It was rather those wretches who crucified him who shackled themselves, cast upon themselves the bonds of their own damnation and, piercing the feet of him who is the way and the life,* do not allow him to reach them. Finally a soldier's lance pierces the side of the innocent one, so that from the heart of innocence a flood of pity might well forth, that watered by it the face of the earth might be restored to fertility. 'Send forth your spirit', he says, 'and they will be created and you shall renew the face of the earth.'* Surely while the author of life gave up his spirit on the cross, from the dead man's pierced side there burst forth the flood of all grace by which the face of the earth has been renewed, that is, the faith of the church, and it has brought forth roses,

*Lk 23:24, cf. Augustine, Hom. in Ps. LIV

*Jn 14:6

*Ps 104:30

lilies of the valley, and gardens of spices.* *Cf. Sg 2:1, 6:1*
The outpouring of the pure blood of Christ, while redeeming the world and washing it from its sins, has brought forth roses in martyrs, lilies in holy virgins, and has produced in perfect preachers gardens of spices. We are, they say, a sweet odor of Christ to God in every place.* What then **2 Co 2:14*
shall we wretches say? What return shall we make to the father of mercies for benefits so great?* We indeed have furnished to his **Cf. Ps 116:12*
only begotten the occasion of his death and our iniquity was the cause of his paying back what he did not steal.* If therefore we **Cf. Ps 69:4*
do not stop doing the deeds for which it is clear he was crucified, do we not as often crucify him again, until he looks at us as we perform the deed for which he had to be crucified. Therefore let us keep the faith, let us imitate his compassion, let us follow righteousness,* and anything we rightly **Cf. 2 Tm 2:22*
censure in others let us through the grace of Christ keep far from ourselves. Perhaps you, my dear friend, had hoped things more suited to your expectations would be written, but meanwhile I had not the grace by which I could offer you more solid fare. Farewell.

LETTER XV

TO

THE ILLUSTRIOUS
COUNTESS OF PERCHE,*

his dear friend in Christ,
brother Adam, sinner,
sends greeting in the Holy Spirit.

---

*The Countess of Perche: probably Mathilde, daughter of Henry the Lion, duke of Saxony and Brunswick, niece of Richard the Lionhearted of England, and sister of the Holy Roman Emperor, Otto IV of Brunswick. Mathilde married Geoffrey II of Perche in 1189, adding to her already illustrious pedigree a connection with the house of Champagne. After Geoffrey's death in 1202, she married Enguerrand III, Lord of Coucy. Adam's letter must therefore to have been written between 1191, the year Geoffrey became Count of Perche, and 1202. Until her death in 1210 she was a benefactoress of the abbey of Perseigne (See Cartulaire de Perseigne, ed. M. Fleury, pp. 96, 98, 205.).

LETTER XV
155

THE URGENCY OF YOUR DEVOTION demands that I should give you by letter advice concerning virtue and should encourage you to long for what is eternal. A happy request indeed and praiseworthy, and would that I had the resources to achieve a happy result. But great is the poverty of soul in someone on whom the unction of the Spirit has not been poured, and he cannot have any other source from which to furnish, for himself or for another, the means of progress. Let us therefore turn to the Holy Spirit in heart and mind; you cling to him by listening and I will draw from him what you may be taught for your soul's health.

156. Oh, what need of a pure and humble mind has he who dedicates himself to be the place where the Holy Spirit works. Surely humility is ready to serve; it keeps far away all the arrogance of pride and it is eager to please the Holy Spirit through pureness of life. Since pride is the source of every sin and, on the contrary, the fear of

the Lord is the beginning of wisdom,* a wise humility carefully sees to it that this remedy confronts that evil. Therefore a humble fear, since it opposes the movements of lofty pride, does not allow the soul to be befouled by sin. He who is without fear will not be justified because when access to the heart is overlooked pride is not kept away from the innermost parts of the soul.

*Ps 111:10, Pr 1:7

157. The virtue of humility expels the heart's pride through the spirit of fear and equally wears down the arrogance of the flesh by the remedy of a holy temperance. Humility is indeed the friend of the Holy Spirit and always prepares for him a spotless dwelling place, but an impure heart does not hesitate to offend him. Upon whom, says the Lord, shall my spirit rest, but on one who is humble and peaceable and who fears my words.* Surely where there is humility there is peace, there is fear and reverence for the commandments.

*Cf. Is 66:2

158. Humility shows you, man, what you are, what you have been, and what you will be hereafter. A little while ago you were nothing. At your beginning you were worthless seed; now you exist a worthless vessel of dung; soon you will be food for worms.

159. Why are you haughty, dust and ashes?* Why do you forget your own condition? Why do you not rather constantly remember that soon you will die? Why do you fix your gaze upon a world which is passing and which as it shakes and crashes

*Si 10:9.
Cf. Gn 18:27,
Si 17:32

constantly threatens its lovers with collapse? Deceitful indeed is its grace and worthless its beauty, for not only do these not bring a long-lived joy, but they fade quickly away into the torment of everlasting lamentation. The things which are transient are not to be loved nor are the things which flee away to be embraced. Rather should devotion be given joyfully to those things which remain for ever. The road to wrong-doing should be blocked, an end be firmly fixed to sin. We should pant after the light of grace that the day of glory and honor may shine upon us. The vanity of a fleeting world must be cast aside, the desire of the deceitful flesh mortified, everything that is in excess pruned away, that a holy temperance may make you adopted as a daughter of God.

160. The spirit of life is sober and admits of no intemperance. It does not sojourn with the soul from which it has seen frugality exiled. It takes no part in dice games. It is not fond of the idle subtlety of chess; the lewd buffoonery of actors agrees not with its own purity. The divine purity does not desire dresses with long trains which serve no purpose except to raise dust and retard the steps of those in a hurry. O unnecessary vanity! O useless display, to deem it inadequate to adorn with expensive care this dungheap of a body unless the dust stirred up be dragged along with a more flowing train. Effeminacy of heart has brought this about to the injury of eyes and ears, because we are

used to stopping our ears and turning away our faces from such dust so elaborately and carefully. Unhappy invention, quite unknown to earlier generations, which hampers one's progress and offends one's sight. It hinders our progress, I say, because the display of useless vanity turns the heart aside from the pursuit of truth. It confuses the vision because through their gazing upon effeminate habits temptation comes upon those who look and turns the eyes of reason from the contemplation of heavenly beauty. O pitiless fashion; that you cover and pile up the dust of the market place with what should cover the nakedness of the poor! The infamous women of our day are not ashamed to be like foxes. Just as those little animals are valued for their long tails, so these women boast of the long trailings of their flowing garments.

161. How often—even worse—clothing of this kind is acquired by robbing the poor, by plundering widows, by taxing orphans. Hence come changes of raiment stretched out on poles, hence expenditure on sumptuous buildings, hence bellies are fattened in elaborate banquets and the worldly nobility has more sumptuous food and costly what-nots drawn from folk who in extreme and unremitting poverty are scarcely living.

162. Would that you, my daughter, might often reflect on this and not, according to the demands of your high birth, be as eager to be conformed to this world as

to study to please him, who as Son of the most high Father willed humbly to be made man on your behalf. Think what you owe to him who created you from nothing and marked you with his own image, stamped you with his likeness, visited you in his incarnation, taught you by his life, redeemed you by his passion, glorified you by his resurrection, raised you on high by his ascension, strengthened you by the grace of his Spirit, the Paraclete. You owe your whole self to him who came so completely to you. Though it is fitting for you to please your husband in the flesh, he nevertheless does not cease duly to seek his right over you.

163. Doubtless though he created soul and body, though he has rights over both, yet meanwhile according to the law of marriage, he has granted your husband rights over your body; but as he claims your soul for himself he does not suffer it to pass over to the right of another. Your husband in the flesh is the spouse of your flesh, but your God is the spouse of your soul. Yet no jealousy moves either of them provided you remain faithful to each and pure. To your heavenly spouse you owe purity of soul, just as to your husband in the flesh you must offer a flesh that is pure. He endowed the purity of your soul with the splendor of the angels and this dowry you received in the mystery of faith and the sureness of hope. O if you love this dowry you will not despise this spouse as if he gave you too small a thing. You are of

noble birth and sprung from royal stock according to the flesh. But you are infinitely more noble from that endowment with which your noble Spouse has invested you. Listen to him, love him, direct your sighs to him, because he is himself the sole sweetness, the supreme beauty, the one joy; and do not because of that other [your husband] deny him his right. And when your fleshly spouse is united with you, you will be delighted that you are spiritually joined to the heavenly one. For he is just, nay, justice itself. He himself has instituted the law of marriage and while you render to each what you know is his, you too are not without part in the heavenly justice. Therefore so offer your husband in your flesh his own right that you do not deprive God his right, for it will not be to your good advantage if you wrongly give the right of the one over to the other.

164. You have been bound to your husband, you are held by necessity to obey him insofar as he lays down nothing contrary to the law of marriage. But in all things must he be preferred who in mortal flesh ordained a wedlock that must pass away and also gave himself to an immortal soul as an immortal spouse. Therefore adorn by the precious cultivation of the virtues that part of yourself in which you have been espoused to Christ, that by the Holy Spirit you may conceive an offspring of good works. Whatever good you speak, whatever good you do, you conceive

wholly by the Holy Spirit, nor can the pure soul be made fruitful from any source other than by the conception of the grace of the Holy Spirit.

165. You need therefore the utmost vigilance that you may keep your heart with all care, if you have dedicated it to be a dwelling-place of the Holy Spirit. If you have not done this, what are you doing? What manner of life are you living? What will you be and how will you bear the day of death soon to come. It will come, it will come and will come quickly, the uncertain hour of certain death, and happy will you be if when it comes it finds you ready. Therefore let your soul be humble, your body chaste, the marriage bed inviolate, your appearance modest, your diet frugal, your countenance reserved, your speech chaste, your hand generous to bestow on the needy according to your means the things they need. Otherwise your marriage cannot be justified, especially since it is granted not by command but by indulgence. Observe that indulgence, not choosing the better part, involves a remedy indeed but does not inherit a reward.

166. Therefore marriage, which was a concession to weakness by means of an indulgence, is instituted as a remedy and is itself useless unless it is safeguarded by the keeping of three good precepts. The first is fidelity, the second hope, the third is called sacrament. Fidelity exists when man and wife so serve each other mutually that they do not cheat one another of the debt

owed to the flesh and so long as they live do not seek a different union. Hope refers to offspring, when they come together with the desire and purpose of instructing their offspring in the sacraments of faith and training them in the knowledge of God. It is called a sacrament when the two living as one flesh so show forth by their unity the likeness of Christ and the church* that for no reason whatever do they seek the separation of such an indissoluble union. If to these three good things which protect marriage from blame you had added works of mercy and piety, if you keep restraint and measure in the lawful activity of the flesh, if you do not unlawfully for the profit of the flesh seize holy days and days of fasting appointed for the profit of the soul, you will not be far from salvation. Mother church has appointed those days, has allotted certain periods for the keeping of fasts, so that whatever fault is committed in the deeds of the flesh, at these times it may be washed away by confession, by prayer, by almsgiving. At these times it is fitting that the soul should be at leisure and see how gentle the Lord is,* and at other times she will discover how foul is the flesh, how worthless the world.

*Cf. Eph 5:31-32

*Cf. Ps 34:8

168. See, my dear friend, you have compelled me to describe for you this principle and if you correct your life by reference to it, you will enhance your glory and increase my joy. May he give you strength, may he keep you, your husband, and your children in all peace and

INDEX TO THE LETTERS

INDEX TO THE LETTERS

Accidie
  103, 108-9, 184
Body of Christ
  76-7, 85-6
Blood of Christ
  83-4, 191
Boredom
  98, 122
Charity
  60, 67, 79, 80, 88-9, 92, 103, 106-7, 112-13, 141, 146-7, 159, 67, 171, 174, 190
Chastity
  57, 75, 80, 91-2, 106
  See also Continence, Virginity
Christ
  53, 79, 81, 83-4, 86-8, 92-3, 103-5, 107, 109-10, 117, 126-7, 130, 134, 142-3, 148-9, 157, 163, 176, 180-1, 184, 188, 190-1, 199, 201
  The Crucified
    53, 185, 187
  Good Shepherd
    85
  Infancy
    75 ff
  Jesus
    58, 80-1, 84-6, 93, 144, 158
  Jesus Christ
    130
  Lamb
    83, 87-8, 106, 188
  Love
    85
  Mediator
    186
  Saviour
    62, 83, 116
  Son of the Most High
    72
  Word
    71, 75-6, 157-9, 190
Church
  53, 84-5, 87, 93, 106, 109, 168, 180, 182, 185, 187, 201
Circumcision
  78-9
Clergy
  182-7
Compunction
  118
  See also Remorse
Contemplation
  69, 101, 118
Contempt of the world
  67, 88
Continence
  107, 177
  See also Chastity, Virginity
Conversion of character (conversio morum)
  108
Conversation
  103, 104, 107-8, 112
Death
  77, 80, 82, 86, 116, 168, 191
Death of Christ
  84-5
  See also Passion of Christ

Index to the Letters

Discipline of life
  67, 106-7, 146
Faith
  81, 100, 107, 146
Fear of the Lord
  100, (107), 113-14, (118), 119, 124-5
Friend(s)
  51, 112, 166 *et passim*
Friendship
  50-51, 66, 70, 112, 122, 152, 166-7, 170
God, attributes of
  61-2, 68, 136
Humility
  84, 103, 105, 109, 127, 155-8, 162, 169, 194-5
Imagination
  69
Intention
  144
Jesus
  See Christ
Leisure
  114, 134, 154-5, 159
Love
  51, 61-2, 66-8, 76, 79, 81, 84, 85-8, 93, 98, 101, 106, 112ff, 118-19, 122, 125, 131, 134-6, 152-5, 162, 166-8
Love, brotherly
  103, 135
Love of neighbor
  103
Marriage (heavenly)
  70, 81, 93, 106, 180-1, 185
Marriage (physical)
  198ff
Martha and Mary
  99, 134
Martin of Tours
  140-9
Martyrdom
  78, 143ff
Mary, B.V.M.
  59-63, 73-7, 157
  Gate of heaven
    72
  Joy of the saints
    72
  Lady of the Angels
    72

Mother of God
  58, 62
Mother of pity
  59, 63
Mother and spouse
  72
Our Lady
  63
Queen of the universe
  72
Star of the sea
  157
Virgin
  71, 74-5, 77, 80, 157, 178
Novices
  99ff, 105-6
Obedience
  76, 82, 100-101, 103, 108, 162
Opus dei
  101-15
Passion of Christ
  80, 82-3, 109, 181, 189-90
  See also Death of Christ
Patience
  82, 109-10
Perseverence
  102, 111, 122
Poverty
  71, 75, 77, 152, 188, 197
Rachel and Bilhah
  69
Rachel and Leah
  99
Reason, human
  176, 178-80
Remorse
  126
  See also Compunction
Rule
  103-4, 108
  Professions according to
    108
Salvation
  53, 105, 136, 201
School of Christ
  144
Scripture(s)
  103-4, 126, 130
Sin, pleasure in
  123-24
Sloth
  102

Index to the Letters

Solitude
   134
Stability
   108, 126
Temptation(s)
   81, 116
Vanity
   51, 105
Virginity
   59, 181
   See also Chastity, Continence

Virtue(s)
   50-52, 59-60, 67, 69-70, 100, 103, 104, 107, 113, 116, 123, 136, 147, 158, 163, 167, 174-6, 183, 194-5
Wisdom
   71, 76-7, 80, 86, 100, 107, 113, 117-18, 124, 136, 154-5, 157-8
Women, womanishness
   54, 159, 182-3, 197
Word
   See Christ

www.ingramcontent.com/pod-product-compliance
Lightning Source LLC
Chambersburg PA
CBHW031415290426
44110CB00011B/393